PENGUIN  CLA

HRAFNKEL'S S

ADVISORY EDITOR: BET

D0404475

Nothing is known of the authorship of *Hrafnkel's Saga*.

•

HERMANN PÁLSSON studied Icelandic at the University of Iceland and Celtic at University College, Dublin. He was formerly Professor of Icelandic at the University of Edinburgh, where he taught from 1950 to 1988. He is the General Editor of the *New Saga Library* and the author of many books on the history and literature of medieval Iceland; his more recent publications include *Legendary Fiction in Medieval Iceland* (with Paul Edwards) and *Art and Ethics in Hrafnkel's Saga*. Hermann Pálsson has also translated (with Magnus Magnusson) *Laxdaela Saga*, *Njal's Saga*, *King Harald's Saga* and *The Vinland Sagas*; and (with Paul Edwards) *Egil's Saga*, *Orkneyinga Saga*, *Eyrbyggja Saga* and *Seven Viking Romances* for Penguin Classics.

HRAFNKEL'S SAGA

and other Icelandic stories

TRANSLATED
WITH AN INTRODUCTION BY
HERMANN PÁLSSON

PENGUIN BOOKS

PENGUIN BOOKS

Published by the Penguin Group
Penguin Books Ltd, 27 Wrights Lane, London W8 5TZ, England
Viking Penguin, a division of Penguin Books USA Inc.
375 Hudson Street, New York, New York 10014, USA
Penguin Books Australia Ltd, Ringwood, Victoria, Australia
Penguin Books Canada Ltd, 2801 John Street, Markham, Ontario, Canada L3R 1B4
Penguin Books (NZ) Ltd, 182–190 Wairau Road, Auckland 10, New Zealand

Penguin Books Ltd, Registered Offices: Harmondsworth, Middlesex, England

This translation first published 1971
10

Copyright © Hermann Pálsson, 1971
All rights reserved

Printed in England by Clays Ltd, St Ives plc
Set in Linotype Baskerville

Audrey-Beth Fitch
Pittsburgh, PA
October 1995

CONTENTS

INTRODUCTION

THE stories in this volume date from the thirteenth century, the Golden Age of saga writing, and they exemplify the outstanding qualities of realistic fiction in medieval Iceland. To begin with, they were written in straightforward natural prose which suits their themes and modes admirably, as the stories deal with lifelike people in credible situations and artificial diction of any kind would have sounded discordant. They belong to a literary tradition which treated familiar themes in a factual manner and accorded the same kind of artistic care and integrity to everyday happenings on a local farm in Iceland as to foreign events of great historic moment. The authors of such stories were constantly aiming at verisimilitude; they made it their business to depict life as they had experienced it, or as they imagined it had actually been in the past. The matter-of-fact style of these stories has led some scholars into the mistaken belief that they are essentially traditional tales which originated mysteriously and miraculously soon after the alleged event (often in the tenth century or slightly later), to be then handed down orally from generation to generation until the scribes in the thirteenth century came along and copied them faithfully down on vellum. But modern scholarship has rejected this simplistic approach to the problem of saga genesis, and it has now been shown that these stories (and others of a similar type) were written in a thirteenth century idiom and by individual authors who were more concerned with moral and aesthetic truths than with historical facts, and who relied more on their own experiences and knowledge of human nature than on the vagaries of popular tradition. It has been pointed out that the realism of these stories is closely related to the purposes for which they were created, for although they have genuine historical settings and later came to be regarded as trustworthy records of actual events, they are nonetheless largely fictional and their relevance to the authors' own times mattered perhaps more than their incidental information about the past. In other words, these stories were not only supposed to throw light on bygone times but also to show up certain facets of human nature and reveal significant strengths and weaknesses in human character. They were, purposively, written in order to conjure up vivid – though not necessarily true – pictures of the past, and at the same time to give the public a clearer vision of the world around them. An important objective of this literature was to encourage people to attain a better understanding of their neighbours and a truer knowledge of themselves, through studying the real and imagined fates of their forebears; a spirit of humanism pervades the narrative. However, this edificatory role was never allowed to get out of hand and dominate the literary art; giving aesthetic pleasure remained the story-writer's primary aim and duty.

The seven stories in the present volume fall into two distinct groups. Three of them – *Hrafnkel's Saga, Thorstein the Staff-Struck* and *Ale-Hood* – are set in the pastoral society of native Iceland, and the remaining four – *Hreidar the Fool, Halldor Snorrason, Audun's Story* and *Ivar's Story* – describe the adventures of Icelandic poets and peasants at the royal courts of Norway and Denmark. The stories in this second group were probably written by authors who had never visited Scandinavia and had therefore no first-hand knowledge of the physical and social background to the incidents they describe, and these stories tell us very little about actual conditions in the countries involved. Their authors were only concerned with the conduct of the Icelandic hero and his relationship with the king he is visiting. The stories about Icelanders at home are very different in this respect. Every incident in them is seen against the backdrop of a familiar landscape, and the realities of Icelandic society are never lost sight of. Place names and other topographical details abound, and this genuineness of the setting contributes to the illusion that the story itself must deal with real events. This is particularly true of *Hrafnkel's Saga*, which evokes some sharply focused landscape images. The depiction of Fljotsdale Moor is, I believe, unique in the entire saga literature. The moor is first described in general terms when Hrafnkel has settled at Adalbol:

> Fljotsdale Moor is stony and boggy and difficult to travel over, yet Hrafnkel and his father used to visit each other frequently, for they were on very affectionate terms, Hallfred thought the usual path across the moor was much too rough, so he looked for an alternative route south of the hills which rise on the moor, and there he found a drier but slightly longer way. This path has been called Hallfredargata ever since, and it can only be used by those who are thoroughly familiar with the moor. (Chapter 2.)

Later in the story (Chapter 18) the moor becomes the scene of action when Eyvind rides across it and Hrafnkel, who is 'thoroughly familiar with the moor', pursues him and eventually catches up with him and kills him. As we follow Eyvind's slow progress over the moor, a clear visual and tactile image of the route gradually emerges:

> There is a swamp there, and one has to ride through watery slush, with the mud reaching up to the horse's knee or mid-leg, sometimes even up to its belly; but underneath the mud the rock is very firm so there's no risk of sinking any deeper. West of

9

this bog the terrain is very stony, and Eyvind and his men rode on to it.

The long, arduous ride continues:

They rode on west across the rocky ground, and then they came to another swamp which is called Oxmire. It's very grassy and has a good many soft patches which make it almost impassable. This bog is about as wide as the previous one but much softer, so that travellers have to dismount. That is why old Hallfred used to take the upper path, even though it was longer; in his opinion these two swamps were almost total barriers. Eyvind and his men rode west into the swamp, and they were so often bogged down they were very much delayed.

And eventually they reach the other side of the moor:

They rode west from the swamp and up the ridge. West of the ridge there's a fine grassy valley, and west of the valley another ridge, and west of the second ridge lies Hrafnkelsdale. They rode up the easternmost ridge. There are some humps on the ridge, and on the slope there stands a steep knoll, with lyme grass on top but eroded by the wind on all sides. This is fine land for grazing, but near it lies a bog. Eyvind rode away from the path and into the hollow east of the lyme knoll. He dismounted and told his companions to let their horses graze there for a while.

To anyone who has travelled on horseback over some of the wilder moors in Iceland this description of Fljotsdale Moor and the ride across it will be vividly familiar, as indeed it must have been to the author's own public. He had clearly come across this particular type of boggy moorland and knew that many of his readers shared in this experience.

In the three stories set in Iceland, the social scene is depicted with no less realism than is the physical background in *Hrafnkel's Saga*. Early Icelandic society was completely rural in character; there were no villages, and the entire population lived on farms and crofts of various sizes, scattered thinly over the inhabitable lowlands and valleys. The distributional pattern of farmsteads goes on the whole back to the Age of Settlements (*c.* 870–*c.* 930), a period which is somewhat romanticized in the first two chapters of *Hrafnkel's Saga*. It is not known how many people immigrated to Iceland during that period or how large the population was in the Middle Ages, but by the end of the eleventh century there were about 4,560 tax-paying farmers in the country, and in the year 1311 the corresponding figure was precisely 3,812. It is not known how many farmers were too poor to pay tax, but their number seems to have been on the increase from the eleventh century onwards, as the Church acquired more and more estates and the class of tenant-farmers expanded. The total size of the population is difficult to guess; in medieval times it can hardly have exceeded eighty thousand, and it may have been smaller, although Iceland is larger in area than Ireland. In 1703, when the first census of the Icelandic population was taken, it was just over 50,330, a considerably lower figure than we would expect for the thirteenth century when our stories were written.

The economy was based on animal husbandry, particularly cattle and sheep, and grass was the most important natural asset. Sheep were kept not only for meat and wool (homespun cloth and other articles made of wool were valuable for export), but also for milk. Transhumance, the seasonal moving of livestock, was widely practised in order to save the precious grassland near the farmstead, and the summer pastures ('the shieling') were often a long distance away. The task of herding the milch ewes (and cows) at the shieling was regarded as a particularly menial job; it was usually assigned to youngsters, and the law made it absolutely clear that no farmer could force his regular farmhands to act as shepherds in summer. It is necessary to bear this in mind when we consider the tragedy of Einar in *Hrafnkel's Saga*. He is far too accomplished a man to be a shepherd in normal circumstances, but he is so desperate that he has no choice in the matter.

Einar in *Hrafnkel's Saga* is engaged to discharge certain prescribed duties (herding the ewes, looking after Freyfaxi and gathering the firewood for the summer), and for this he gets his keep for a whole year. A regular farmhand would be rewarded more generously; the wages he was entitled to were determined by law. Only well-to-do (tax-paying) farmers like Hrafnkel, Sam and Bjarni in *Hrafnkel's Saga* and Bjarni of Hof in *Thorstein the Staff-Struck*, could afford hired hands, but the stories also show us peasants who were so badly off that they were entirely dependent on the cheap labour provided by their children. To that type belong the ex-viking Thorarin in *Thorstein the Staff-Struck* who 'had little money, but a good many weapons', and Thorbjorn in *Hrafnkel's Saga* who 'had slender means but a large family to support'. Peasants of this type were quite common in Iceland from medieval times down to the twentieth century, but it seems unlikely that there could have been many of them in the first half of the tenth century when *Hrafnkel's Saga* is supposed to have taken place. At that time, wealth was much more evenly distributed than later. The depiction of Thorbjorn's poverty seems to reflect conditions in the thirteenth century, and the same applies to many other social aspects in these stories. The poorest peasants used to lead a very precarious existence, and were never far from starvation. This kind of hardship is clearly understood by the author of *Hrafnkel's Saga*, but it is never more deeply felt than when Thorbjorn tells his son Einar why he must look for a job elsewhere:

The reason is, I can run the farm with the help of my other children, and a man of your ability should find it easy enough to get a job. It's not for any lack of love that I'm sending you away, I love you more than my other children, but I have been driven to this by my poverty and lack of means. My other children are getting big enough for work now and you'll be able to get better employment than they ever could.

As soon as Thorbjorn's younger children are old enough for work, Einar becomes in fact a liability, as the farm is too small to feed more than a limited number of mouths. There is a note of bitterness in Thorbjorn's words when he mentions the poverty that rules his life and forces him to drive his son away. The theme of poverty is taken up again by Hrafnkel when Thorbjorn asks him for compensation for Einar. Hrafnkel genuinely regrets what he has done and wants to make amends by freeing Thorbjorn from the bondage of poverty:

I'll supply your household with plenty of milk in the summer and meat in the autumn, and I'll keep on doing this every year for as long as you choose to live on your farm. I'll also provide for your sons and daughters to give them a good start in life. And from now on you need only tell me if there's anything in my possession which you want and you'll have it and never have to do without. You can keep on farming for as long as you like, but move over here and stay with me when you tire of it, and I'll look after you for the rest of your life.

Hrafnkel's offer is as generous as it is apposite in the circumstances, for he wants to mitigate the misery that forced Thorbjorn to send his son away. The offer implies that Thorbjorn is too destitute to make certain that his family has always enough to eat, and that it is beyond his means to help his children get started in life. Later in the story, Hrafnkel himself is stripped of all his wealth and power, so that he is reduced to the same state of poverty as Thorbjorn. But Hrafnkel has the courage and good luck to make his way back to power and prosperity.

The situation at Sunnudale in *Thorstein the Staff-Struck* is so precarious that the welfare of the household depends entirely on young Thorstein, 'who worked so hard on his father's farm that three other men could hardly have done better'. Without him, the family would starve, which explains why the local chieftain is so reluctant to enforce the sentence of outlawry after Thorstein has been convicted of manslaughter. Bjarni 'simply isn't prepared to take the only breadwinner at Sunnudale away from Thorstein's blind father and other dependants there'. It is his obvious duty as a chieftain to think of the welfare of his poverty-stricken neighbours, and this duty is clearly acknowledged by Hrafnkel as we have seen already.

Practically every scene in the three stories set in Iceland has a familiar social setting, and it is this homely touch that gives the incidents such a strong feeling of immediacy. Here we see a shepherd setting out early one morning to search the desolate moors for his straying sheep, and we get a glimpse of the dairy maids milking the ewes at the shieling the following morning; then there is a servant washing her laundry by the lakeside; a charcoal maker dozing off one night beside the smouldering embers and accidentally setting fire to the wooded countryside; two farm-hands pitting their horses against one another in a fight; a hardworking peasant coming back into the living room one winter morning to rest after feeding the cattle. Thus the stories keep evoking fleeting images of rural activity, but mixed with these are acts of violence and injustice. Disruptive forces keep obtruding and shattering the peaceful pattern of everyday life: the shepherd finds his missing sheep, but the curtain falls abruptly on the pastoral idyll when he is murdered by the man he is working for. The servant down by the lake does not bother to finish her washing but rushes home to her master to urge him to kill an innocent traveller who has just ridden past. The charcoal maker soon becomes the intended victim of corrupt chieftains who are determined to turn his accident into a

lucrative court case. And the horse-fight ends in a brawl
which leads to the death of one of the peasants and turns
the other into a reluctant killer.

Law-breaking is a common theme in the Icelandic sagas,
and there are several instances of punishable acts in our
stories. The chieftain-farmer in *Hrafnkel's Saga* who brut-
ally murders his shepherd (not the first shepherd in world
literature to become an innocent victim) is then harshly
punished for his crime. But the punishment is not an un-
qualified triumph of justice, for Hrafnkel's opponents have
no scruples in resorting to violence and unlawful acts
themselves: they deny him the right to defend himself before the judges and use force to keep him out of court when
his case is being heard. And their torture of him is not only
a gross offence against human dignity but also a criminal
act. Later in the story, Hrafnkel takes a cruel revenge on
one of his tormentors, but by that time he has become so
powerful that no one can curb him, and his second killing
goes unpunished. *Ale-Hood* describes a man who accidentally destroys some woodland belonging to six chieftains,
and since there is no criminal intent involved he should
only be liable to compensate the owners for the actual loss.
However, they decide to prosecute him for arson in the
hope of convicting him as a criminal so that they can con-
fiscate his property, which is what happens to Hrafnkel
after he has been sentenced to outlawry at the Althing. In
Hrafnkel's Saga and *Ale-Hood* most of the chieftains are
presented in an unfavourable light, for they fail in their
primary duty to guard the integrity of the law. Hrafnkel
regards himself above the law and tramples on the rights
of others, and the six avaricious chieftains in *Ale-Hood* are
eager to manipulate the law in order to make some money.
The only ideal chieftain is Bjarni of Hof in *Thorstein the
Staff-Struck*; after Thorstein has killed three of his farmhands and been sentenced to outlawry for manslaughter,

Bjarni stubbornly and nobly tempers justice with mercy, and eventually the two men are reconciled.

There can be little doubt that the author of *Hrafnkel's Saga* had in mind contemporary chieftains when he described the hero of the story. In the thirteenth century Iceland endured several tyrannical and powerful chieftains who had the backing of the Church and of the Crown of Norway and who ruthlessly imposed their will on other chieftains and farmers and even on the Althing itself. In spite of that Hrafnkel is also endowed with certain tenth century features: he is a pagan priest and a fervent worshipper of the god Frey. These pagan elements show the author's keen antiquarian interest, and they add to the verisimilitude of *Hrafnkel's Saga*. They helped the public to accept the story as a record of tenth century events. By the thirteenth century, the pagan period had become very remote and most saga authors felt no aversion to romanticizing it. There is of course no reason to believe that the author of *Hrafnkel's Saga* knew any traditions about Hrafnkel's pagan practices. In fact he seems to have had no information about the historical Hrafnkel beyond what he could glean from the *Book of Settlements* (see n. 2, p. 36 below). The place name *Freyfaxahamar*[1] and the severe legal penalties for horse-stealing may have given him the idea of the forbidden horse.

The pagan elements in *Hrafnkel's Saga* are, however, incongruous in one respect: they clash sharply with the tightly woven pattern of Christian ethics that gives the whole story such a distinctive character and cohesion. *Hrafnkel's Saga* has been called 'an essay in guilt', a description that accentuates the salient differences between this type of novel-like saga on the one hand, and the primi-

1. 'Freyfaxi's Bluff'; *Freyfaxi* can only be the name of a horse dedicated to Frey. The place has not been identified.

tive heroic tradition, embodied in the pagan poetry and the adventure sagas, on the other. In the heroic literature, inexorable fate plays a decisive role; the hero lives out his life according to a predestined pattern. The forces of destiny are too strong for any mortal to defy and the hero must accept the fate allotted him by God or a pagan deity. Furthermore, in such poems and sagas, divine power not only controls the fates of men but also the forces of nature whose laws can be suspended at will. But *Hrafnkel's Saga* shows hardly any trace of belief in predestination, and the story is completely naturalistic apart from the prophetic dream in Chapter One which, it should be noted, the author borrowed from another literary source. In the realistic sagas, the characters are no longer the pawns of fate but their actions are seen as manifestations of their free will. Each individual is responsible for what he does and, within the limits circumscribed by his innate talents and external factors such as poverty and unfavourable social position, he is responsible for his own fate. What matters most is that people should use their freedom of choice for the benefit of themselves and others, and a failure to do this can lead to tragedy. The character who enjoys the greatest freedom of all in *Hrafnkel's Saga*, the wealthy and talented Hrafnkel, misuses it in a number of ways, to his own and others' detriment. His fatal mistake is that he deliberately curbs his own freedom of action by swearing an oath to kill anyone who rides Freyfaxi without his permission, so that in one particular contingency he must act in a certain predetermined way. Einar is also a talented man, but his freedom of action is severely restricted by his poverty, and his father narrows that limited freedom even further by failing to warn him in time to seek employment elsewhere. Because of his father's improvidence there is apparently no vacancy left for him except to be Hrafnkel's shepherd, and that particular job involves the forbidden horse. But it is finally left to Einar himself to take the irrevocable step that leads to his death. He misuses his freedom of choice when he yields to temptation and rides Freyfaxi. The shepherd's fall is no sudden impulse but a premeditated act and he is made to pay the ultimate penalty for it. The shepherd's tragedy is clearly inspired by the story of the Fall in Genesis, which in medieval times was used to exemplify moral problems connected with the freedom of the will, temptation and disobedience.[2] As in the Biblical model, the tempted is warned on pain of death not to touch the forbidden thing. but apart from that he is given a wide choice:

'Some ten or twelve other horses go with Freyfaxi and you're free to use any of them, whenever you like, by day or night. I want you never to ride this horse for ... I've sworn an oath to kill anyone who rides him.'	You may eat indeed of all the trees in the garden. Nevertheless of the tree of the knowledge of good and evil you are not to eat, for on the day you eat of it you shall most surely die.[3]
'Why did you ride this one horse which was forbidden you, when there were plenty of other horses you were free to ride?'	Have you been eating of the tree I forbade you to eat? ... What is this you have done?[4]

In *Hrafnkel's Saga* the death threat is interpreted literally, and the shepherd's master carries it out without any hesitation, it seems. But the shepherd's transgression in no way exculpates Hrafnkel from the guilt of murder, as he himself had created the situation by swearing the fatal oath, and even afterwards it was within his power to vio-

2. *Hrafnkel's Saga* has several other allusions to the Bible, but this one seems to me particularly significant.

3. *The Jerusalem Bible* (Darton, Longman & Todd, 1966), p. 16.

4. ibid., p. 18.

late the oath and spare Einar's life. But once the crime has been committed, other people keep aggravating the situation by immoderate action. Thorbjorn shows a tragic lack of self-knowledge[5] when he rejects Hrafnkel's offer of compensation and insists on referring the issue to arbitration which, as Hrafnkel points out, would make them equals. The subsequent torture of Hrafnkel and Sam's failure to have him put to death and be on his guard against him[6] precipitate Hrafnkel's second crime: the killing of Eyvind. Throughout the story we keep meeting people who, in the sense of medieval values, are guilty of pride and who wilfully make life harder than necessary for everyone concerned. But nowhere is there any attempt to blame the tragedy on the forces of destiny.

Hrafnkel's Saga and the other stories in this volume owe much to the humanistic tradition of the Middle Ages. They are concerned with human emotions and sufferings and in them human dignity is taken for granted, irrespective of social position and wealth. The stories describe people who are in some way vulnerable. It is a far cry from the heroic poetry in the *Edda* with its idealized ethos and its strong emphasis on aristocratic background, fatalism, personal honour and physical courage, to the stark realism with which the Icelandic farmers and farmhands are described in our stories. In the realistic sagas there is no place for the heroic exploits, and sometimes one can detect a marked anti-heroic sentiment which would have been unthinkable in the ancient poems about the valorous deeds of the Volsungs and other larger-than-life warriors of royal and divine stock. This sentiment is particularly prominent in *Thorstein the Staff-Struck*, where old Thorarin typifies the traditional warrior-hero. His principal assets are an assortment of weapons from his fighting days and the

5. 'He's a wise man who knows himself.'
6. 'One must always watch out for the wicked.'

rigid obsolescent ideas of honour and blood-revenge that inevitably go with such possessions. He is a fossilized relic from the Viking past and he fails to integrate into the peaceful rural community of which he is a reluctant and useless member. In contrast, his son is hard-working and peaceable and devotes his life to the welfare of his family. The story describes a clash between two moral codes, and it is the new spirit of peace that triumphs in the end over the old ideals of the warrior past. The retired viking who feels so strongly about honour that he would rather have a dead son than one who is considered a coward, has no qualms about resorting to trickery when he wants to avenge his son. Bjarni's two servants who ridicule him for his failure to take revenge on Thorstein belong to the same school, and ironically, they get themselves killed, when they try to vindicate their master's reputation. Bjarni's wife at first urges revenge, but she tries to hold him back once she realizes that he is intending to offer his opponent fair play and fight him in single combat. The old heroic attitudes are nowhere expressed more forcefully than in *Hrafnkel's Saga* when the washing-woman lectures her master on the over-riding duty of revenge:

'The old saying is true enough, "The older a man, the feebler." The honour a man's given early in life isn't worth much, if he has to give it all up in disgrace, and hasn't the courage to fight for his rights ever again. It's a peculiar thing indeed to happen to those who were once thought brave. As for those who grew up with their father, it's a different story, for as soon as they reached manhood they went abroad, travelling from country to country, and when they come back they're thought very highly of, even above chieftains. Eyvind Bjarnason was just crossing the river at Skala Ford carrying a bright shield that shone in the sun. He's a worthy target for revenge, an outstanding man like him.'

To this outspoken exponent of heroic morality, it does

not matter in the least that Eyvind Bjarnason is completely
innocent. It is indeed the awareness of his own innocence
that prevents Eyvind from saving his life when Hrafnkel
pursues him: 'I'm not going to run away from someone
I've never wronged.' Hrafnkel himself belongs to the old
heroic school; killing people comes easily to him and he
has no scruples about offering his victims unfair odds: the
shepherd is unarmed and makes no attempt to defend himself when Hrafnkel strikes him down with an axe, and
Hrafnkel sets out after Eyvind with a much stronger force
than Eyvind has. But Hrafnkel is also capable of compro-
mise, he prefers to live in humiliation rather than die with
honour.

What matters most in these stories is not external action,
but rather motives and emotions, why people behave in
the way they do and how they feel. The last story in the
present volume deals with a situation that is very familiar
to saga readers. The opening of *Ivar's Story* is a variation
on a well-known theme which is treated differently in *Laxdæla Saga*[7], *Gunnlaug's Saga* and *Bjorn's Saga*, and could
be summarized as follows: an Icelander travels abroad,
leaving behind the girl he loves, and she is supposed to
wait for his return. With him is another Icelander who has
set his heart on the same girl, and soon the two suitors fall
out. The girl's lover stays behind in Norway but the other
goes back to Iceland and wins her hand by telling her a
false story about the man she loves. This is also basically
the situation in *Ivar's Story* but the similarities end there
and the three sagas I mentioned have a different sequel:
the jealous husband kills the hero after he comes back to
Iceland and the wife has discovered that she has been
tricked into marrying the wrong man; in *Gunnlaug's Saga*
the hero and the husband kill each other. In *Ivar's Story*
the deceitful husband is the hero's brother, and he seems to

7. Penguin Classics, 1969.

be motivated by envy and malice rather than by love; once
he has married the woman he fades completely out of the
story. The woman plays no active part, and she is hardly
more than a symbol, whereas in the three sagas I mentioned love is treated romantically and the woman contributes significantly to the tragedy. *Ivar's Story* is mainly
concerned with pain and mitigation, the anguish caused
by the loss of the woman and the subsequent remedy for it.
The king notices Ivar's unhappiness and sets about diag-
nosing its cause with remarkable insight, and once he has
discovered what is wrong with Ivar, he starts making him
tempting offers of women, wealth and social advancement.
But like the steadfast pilgrim hero in *Audun's Story* Ivar
resists the temptation and only accepts the one cure that
fits the situation. The remedy is only possible when the
physician has shared with the sufferer the knowledge of
the nature of the pain.

In *Hrafnkel's Saga* the theme of pain is given a more
sophisticated treatment, and the suffering is more ruthlessly administered and more poignantly felt. But there, the
human situation is also more complex and the pattern of
motivation more intricate. The principal exponent of pain
and suffering is the destitute farmer, Thorbjorn, whose
favourite son is murdered by his powerful neighbour,
Hrafnkel. These two men are not only contrasted in terms
of social position and wealth but also by the objects of their
love. Thorbjorn loves his son deeply, but Hrafnkel is
moved by a passionate love for the god Frey and the horse
Freyfaxi. This emotional difference is closely related to the
theme of pain. Hrafnkel kills the son Thorbjorn loves so
dearly, and as the result Hrafnkel himself loses the god and
the horse that were so dear to him. But whereas Thorbjorn
suffers an irreparable loss in the death of his son, Hrafnkel
gains by losing the objects of his love; without Frey and
Freyfaxi he becomes a freer man than before. He sums this

up himself when he learns that Freyfaxi has been killed: 'I think it's a vain thing to believe in the gods.' Thorbjorn's grief is aggravated by his failure to take revenge and bring Hrafnkel to justice, and a year after the murder he breaks down weeping at the Althing. But then suddenly the mood of the story changes, when a complete stranger, Thorkel, enters the scene and takes an interest in his case. He says it is necessary to gain the help of his brother Thorgeir, a powerful chieftain. Thorgeir has been suffering from a nasty boil on his foot and is now sound asleep. Thorkel tells Thorbjorn to go up to him and pull hard at the sore toe. Predictably, Thorgeir is furious when he is wakened by the pain.

Then Thorkel stepped into the booth and said to his brother Thorgeir, 'Don't be so quick to lose your temper over this, kinsman, for you'll come to no harm. People's actions are often worse than their intentions, and they find it particularly difficult to pay full attention to everything when they have a lot on their minds. Your excuse, kinsman, is that your foot is tender and it's given you a lot of trouble. That's a pain only you can feel. It could be that an old man won't feel any less suffering over the death of his son, particularly since he has no means of redress and is completely helpless. That's a pain only he can feel. It stands to reason that someone with so much on his mind can't be expected to pay full attention to things.'

Thorkel wants to rouse his brother's sympathy for Thorbjorn and in order to do this he tries first to establish a bond of fellow-suffering between Thorbjorn and him. It is by sharing in other people's pain that we are moved to compassion and pity. But as it turns out, Thorgeir is callously impervious to this argument and only promises his help after his brother has threatened to abandon him. Later in the story, the theme of pain is resumed when Hrafnkel is tortured in order to bring home to him the sufferings he has caused other people in the past. He is thus given a harsh lesson in compassion, and the experience of pain makes him milder and gentler to begin with, but when his servant urges him to take revenge his sense of pity is easily blunted. After Hrafnkel has killed Eyvind he argues with a good deal of justification that Sam has suffered no more in the death of his brother than Hrafnkel himself did when he was tortured. Thus the author keeps equating the two different kinds of suffering: physical pain and mental anguish.

The pathetic picture of old Thorbjorn, helpless and weeping that summer morning at the Althing, has a striking parallel in *Ale-Hood*, though the circumstances are also very different in some respects. Ale-Hood has few things in his favour and is not the kind of person who normally invokes our sympathy: a mean, ugly man, rich and boastful. Like Thorbjorn he is arrogant, sadly lacking in self-knowledge, and he has himself partly to blame for the situation. It is only when he has given up hope at the Althing and broken down weeping, a forlorn figure no one seems to pity, that an unexpected helper turns up and saves him. Ale-Hood gets his reward once his pride has been curbed and he has attained enough self-knowledge to be moved to tears.

The structure of *Hrafnkel's Saga* is neater than that of any other Icelandic saga. After a brief descriptive Prologue (Chs. 1–3) it falls into three acts which could be called *Murder* (4–6), *Punishment* (7–16) and *Revenge* (17–19); this is followed by a short Epilogue which rounds off the story (20). The climax of Acts I and II is a violent deed: the murder of the shepherd (I), and the torture and humiliation of Hrafnkel (II); but in Act III there are two climaxes: the killing of Eyvind which corresponds to the shepherd's murder in Act I, and the humiliation of Sam which echoes the treatment of Hrafnkel in Act II. In each

Act there are two crucial scenes set on a summer's morning: the shepherd's fall and his death at the shieling the following morning (I); Thorkel's intervention at the Althing, and the torture of Hrafnkel at Adalbol a fortnight later (II); Eyvind's fatal ride across the moor, and Sam's eviction from Adalbol the following morning (III). The structure is strengthened by an effective use of parallelisms and contrasts, both in the delineation of character and the arrangement of scenes and situations. As an example of this one could mention the prelude to the two killings. On both occasions a serving woman exchanges some words with Hrafnkel, and as the result of what he learns from her, Hrafnkel sets out in a murderous mood: 'In the morning he had a horse brought in and saddled, and rode up to the shieling. He was wearing blue clothing and carrying an axe in his hand, and that was the only weapon he had.' When Hrafnkel goes after Eyvind, he and his men 'armed themselves resolutely', but it is through the eyes of Eyvind's servant boy that we get a vivid picture of Hrafnkel: 'There are some men riding after us, eighteen or twenty of them. One of the riders is a tall man wearing blue clothing and he seems to me very like Hrafnkel, though I've not set eyes on him for quite a long time.' The image of Hrafnkel riding in blue clothing tells us precisely all we need to know about his mood and intentions, for in the sagas blue clothing is conventionally worn by killers.[8] The two victims have several features in common, apart from being cousins: both are killed innocently, though they are also at fault: Einar for taking the forbidden horse

8. It should be noted that the Icelandic word for blue (blá-r) had a much wider range of meaning than its English cognate and counterpart. It denoted every shade of blue and black, and was used to describe not only the colour of the clear sky but also that of the raven. This was the colour particularly associated with *Hel*, the Goddess of Death, which may partly account for the literary convention of dressing killers in blue.

and Eyvind for being too proud to save his life. But there are also striking contrasts: Einar is poor and is slaughtered like a sacrificial lamb, whereas the wealthy and far-travelled Eyvind puts up a brave fight before he is killed. Einar is buried unceremoniously with a heap of stones to mark his grave, but Eyvind is given a proper burial mound. Einar's name is commemorated by that simple cairn, but Eyvind's by a mountain and other impressive features of the landscape. The contrasts between Hrafnkel and Sam are also memorably drawn, and it was a particularly clever move on the author's part to make Hrafnkel use Sam's speech at Adalbol as the basis for his when their fortunes are reversed.

The stories with Scandinavian settings describe situations which were alien and unfamiliar to the Icelandic public for whom they were written: happenings at a royal court. From the late eleventh century onwards Icelandic antiquarians and historians spent a great deal of time and vellum on the history of the kings of Norway and Denmark[9] and this led inevitably to an interest in the Icelan-

9. The first Icelander to write on the history of the kings of Norway (in Latin) was Sæmund Sigfusson (1056–1133). His work is now lost, but references to him show that he dealt among other things with the rulers of Norway from Harald Fine-Hair (late ninth and early tenth centuries) to Magnus the Good (d. 1047). It is not known when Sæmund began his work, but it was presumably after he came back to Iceland (c. 1076) from France where he had been studying for a number of years. He was soon followed by other historians: Ari Thorgilsson (1068–1148), Eirik Oddsson, Odd Snorrason, Karl Jonsson (d. 1213), Gunnlaug Leifsson (d. 1218 or 1219), Styrmir Karason (d. 1245), Snorri Sturluson (1179–1241), and Sturla Thordarson (1214–84). They all wrote in Icelandic, except Sæmund, Odd and Gunnlaug; all of them were priests or monks except Snorri and Sturla. Apart from these authors, there were others whose names are unknown. *Morkinskinna* (written about 1220), one of these anonymous histories of the kings of Norway, contains among other

dic court poets and other adventurers who had served or
visited the kings concerned. A favourite theme in such
stories is a tension between the king and his Icelandic
guest, and the two characters juxtaposed are often very different from one another. An exception from this is *Ivar's
Story* (see above, pp. 21–2), where the two men are shown
as friends and the king acts as a spiritual adviser to the Icelander. This Ivar [Ingimundarson] is a historical personage; several fragments of his eulogies on the kings of
Norway still survive. *Hreidar the Fool*, on the other hand,
describes a half-witted peasant who seems to be completely
fictional, the author's own creation. Hreidar goes to Norway where he meets the two ruling kings and clowns his
way through some sticky situations. He is a placid man and
his great ambition is to find out what it really means to
lose one's temper, but the actual experience comes as a
great shock to him, and he kills a man in a rage. After his
escapades in Norway he goes back to Iceland, a better man
than before. The story exemplifies an idea used elsewhere
in the saga literature, that any person is bound to be improved by associating with good people, and King Magnus
the Good is one of those rare people whose mere presence
has beneficial effects on others. *Halldor Snorrason* describes a sustained conflict between the crafty King Harald
Hardradi and an honest, outspoken Icelander who has
served the king for a long time and finally lost faith in
him. Halldor represents a type much admired by saga
authors: the person who refuses to yield an inch to his
superior when he knows he has justice on his side, even if
it means risking his life. The scene where Halldor forces
King Harald at the point of a sword to give him his full
pay is one of the most memorable moments in the vast
literature relating to the lives of the kings of Norway, and

---

stories *Halldor Snorrason, Audun's Story* (though not the version
translated here) and *Ivar's Story*.

Halldor Snorrason has sometimes been described as the ideal Icelandic hero: the independent farmer who fights for his rights to the bitter end, who fears nothing and allows nothing to disturb his equanimity and composure. Halldor is a real historical personage. As the story claims, he went back to Iceland and started farming at Hjardarholt, where some of the protagonists in the tragic *Laxdæla Saga* had lived before him.

Audun's Story is one of the most brilliant pilgrim stories in world literature. The hero is a farmhand in the west of Iceland who gets the opportunity to go abroad and see the world. He travels first to Norway and then to Greenland where he spends all his money on buying a polar bear. Then he returns to Scandinavia and gives the bear as a present to King Svein Ulfsson of Denmark.[10] The king rewards him generously so that Audun is able to complete his pilgrimage to Rome. When he comes back to Denmark, King Svein tempts him with splendid offers to stay with him, but Audun steadfastly turns them down and hurries back to Iceland to take care of his mother who would become a pauper should he fail to return. This is a story about a man's loyalty to his own integrity, and through his own efforts Audun becomes a man of good luck.

The stories in this volume are anonymous, but it has been suggested that *Hrafnkel's Saga* was probably written by Abbot Brand Jónson (d. 1264), one of the leading intellectuals in thirteenth century Iceland. He was for a number of years head of the Augustinian monastery at

10. Polar bears were highly prized as gifts in medieval times. We know from a reliable historical source (*Hungrvaka*) that Isleif Gizurarson, the first native bishop of Iceland, presented the Holy Emperor with a Greenland bear about the year 1054. The early Icelandic laws mention polar bears being kept as pets, and these were probably brought from Greenland, though polar bears occasionally visit Iceland by the drift ice.

Thykkvaby (1247–62), and finally Bishop of Hólar (1262–64). Contemporary sources refer to him as an outstanding Church leader, teacher and peace-maker; he acted as a successful mediator and arbitrator in several bitter disputes. But it is for his contributions to Icelandic letters that his name is chiefly remembered. Medieval manuscripts accredit him with two works of considerable importance. One is the so-called *Gyðinga Saga* ('History of the Jews'), which is based on several learned sources: the *Antiquitates Judaicae* and *De Bello Judaico* of Flavius Josephus (d.c.100), the *Historia Scholastica* of Peter Comestor (d.1179 or 1189), and the Bible. The Icelandic version was probably completed before Brand took charge of the monastery in 1247, since the manuscript attributes it to 'Brand Jónsson, *the Priest*, who later became Bishop of Hólar'. About 1260 Abbot Brand made a brilliant prose version in Icelandic of the twelfth century Latin epic *Alexandreis* of Philippe Gautier de Châtillon (d. after 1184). Abbot Brand's translation, *Alexander's Saga*, is one of the great literary monuments of medieval Iceland. It has been shown that there are some notable stylistic affinities between *Hrafnkel's Saga* and the two works attributed to Abbot Brand; the verbal parallels between *Hrafnkel's Saga* and *Alexander's Saga* are particularly striking. It has also been suggested that the characterization of Hrafnkel may have been influenced by the depiction of Alexander in the Latin epic.

Abbot Brand belonged to the Freysgydling family (see p. 37, n. 4, below), and there can be little doubt that *Hrafnkel's Saga* was written for or by a member of that family. The story seems to reflect a series of tragic happenings that overtook the Freysgydlings during the period 1248 to 1255; *Hrafnkel's Saga* was probably written during the last year or two of Abbot Brand's life. Briefly, the most significant parallels between these mid-thirteenth century events and the saga are as follows: Abbot Brand's brother-in-law, Ogmund Helgason of Kirkjuby (who corresponds to Hrafnkel), a powerful and domineering farmer, clashed violently with Abbot Brand's nephew, Sæmund Ormsson (who corresponds to Sam in the saga). Sæmund was young and ambitious, and like Sam, he had to get the support of a powerful man from the west of Iceland to overcome his adversary. On one occasion at the Althing when neither Ogmund nor Abbot Brand were present, so that there was no one to defend Ogmund, Sæmund with the help of his ally from the west had Ogmund sentenced to outlawry. Subsequently, Sæmund held a court of confiscation on Ogmund, making him completely penniless. However, Abbot Brand intervened and managed to reconcile them; he warned Sæmund strongly not to break the agreement and trusted that Ogmund would honour it on his part. But the abbot lived to regret this advice, because Ogmund did not keep his word. He ambushed Sæmund and his brother Gudmund (who has been compared with Eyvind), and killed them both. There are also a number of minor but suggestive details in *Hrafnkel's Saga* which seem to support the claim that the story is based on contemporary events. In *Hrafnkel's Saga*, Eyvind and his men wear coloured clothing; from a near-contemporary source[11] we know precisely how Sæmund and his brother Gudmund were attired: Sæmund was wearing a red and green tunic, and Gudmund a blue one, and each of them had a cloak of different colour. This detail is worth noticing since we know that Abbot Brand saw his nephews' bodies the day they were killed, and their elegant clothing is not likely to have slipped his memory easily. The brothers were killed on a Saturday, and Eyvind is evidently also supposed to have lost his life on the same day of the week as we

11. *Svinfellinga Saga.* Some of these thirteenth century events are also mentioned in *Islendinga Saga* of Sturla Thordarson (1214–84).

can see from the fact that a woman is washing in the lake.[12]

The identity of the author of *Hrafnkel's Saga* will probably never be established beyond all reasonable doubt, but whatever his name was, the story shows us clearly that he must have been a man of exceptional sensitivity and understanding – one of the humanists and humanizers of thirteenth century Iceland.

12. The Icelandic words for Saturday (*laugar-dagr* or *þváttdagr*), mean literally 'bath-day' or 'washing-day'.

NOTE ON THE TRANSLATION

THIS translation of *Hrafnkel's Saga* is based on a paper MS dating from the early seventeenth century (AM 551C, 4to)[1]; this MS is defective, and the gaps have been filled from a copy written at the beginning of the eighteenth century when it was in a better state than now (AM 451, 4to). However, several doubtful readings in this version have been replaced by passages from other seventeenth century MSS (AM 156, fol., AM 158, fol. and AM 443, 4to). Apart from a single leaf on vellum, the saga survives only in paper MSS. There exists no definitive edition of *Hrafnkel's Saga*, but the best printed version of it is Jón Helgason's edition in the *Nordisk Filologi* series: *Hrafnkel's Saga Freysgoða*, Ejnar Munksgaard, Copenhagen, 1950. (It has been reprinted several times since.) A critical edition of the saga, based on all the known MSS is now being prepared by Peter Springborg for the *Editiones Arnamagnæanæ* series. The chapter division of the saga in the present translation is based on Helgason's edition, but the chapter headings are my own.

Thorstein the Staff-Struck ('Þorsteins þáttr stangarhöggs'), *Ale-hood* (Ölkofra þáttr'), *Halldor Snorrason* (Halldórs þáttr Snorrasonar') and *Hreidar the Fool* ('Hreiðars þáttr heimska') are translated from the text in the *Íslenzk Fornrit* series (vols. XI, V, X). *Audun's Story* ('Auðunar þáttr vestfirzka') is taken from the version preserved in *Flateyjarbók* (edited by Guðbrandr Vigfússon and C. R. Unger, 1859–68), and *Ivar's Story* ('Ivars þáttr

1. Preserved in the Arnamagnæan Library in Copenhagen.

Note on the Translation

Ingimundarsonar') from *Morkinskinna* (edited by Finnur Jónsson, 1932).

All the stories in the volume have been translated before, and a number of books and articles have been written about them. For editions, previous translations and other works relating to these stories, see *ISLANDICA* (Cornell University Press), vols. I, III, XXIV, XXVI and XXXVIII, and *BIBLIOGRAPHY of Old Norse-Icelandic Studies*, Munksgaard, Copenhagen, 1963–.

It is my pleasant duty to thank my friends Professor Denton Fox and Paul Edwards M.A. for reading the translation in manuscript and weeding out a good many infelicities and inaccuracies that otherwise would have marred this book. I am also greatly indebted to Mrs Betty Radice and Miss Julia Vellacott for scrutinizing the final version of the text and making many valuable suggestions.

Hermann Pálsson
Edinburgh, June 1969

HRAFNKEL'S SAGA

1. THE IMMIGRANTS

IT was in the days of King Harald Fine-Hair[1] that a man
called Hallfred brought his ship to Iceland, putting in
at Breiddale east of the Fljotsdale District. On board were
his wife and their fifteen-year-old son Hrafnkel, a handsome and promising youngster.

Hallfred built himself a home. The following winter a
foreign bondwoman called Arnthrud died there, and that
is why the place has been known as Arnthrudarstead ever
since. In the spring Hallfred moved house north across the
moor and made his new home at Geitdale.

One night he dreamed that a man came to him and said,
'There you lie, Hallfred, but that's not a prudent thing to
do. Move house west across Lagarwater, your good luck
awaits you there.' Then he woke up.

He moved house west to the other side of Rang River in
Tongue, to a place which is now known as Hallfredarstead,
and lived there till old age. But he happened to leave behind a male goat and a barren she-goat, and on the very
day he moved out, a landslide fell on the farmstead killing
these two beasts, which is why this place has been called
Geitdale ever since.

1. *The son of Helfdan the Black, the son of Gudrod the Hunter-
King, the son of Halfdan 'the Open-Handed but Inhospitable', the
son of Eystein Fart, the son of Olaf the Wood-Cutter, king of the
Swedes.* This remarkable genealogy occurs in several sources, and the
author of *Hrafnkel's Saga* probably borrowed it from Ari Thorgilsson's *Islendingabók*. According to Icelandic reckoning King
Harald Fine-Hair died in 931 or 932.

2. THE YOUNG CHIEFTAIN

Hrafnkel made it his custom in the summer to go riding
over the moors. At that time Jokulsdale had been fully
settled as far up as the bridge. When Hrafnkel was riding
across Fljotsdale Moor he saw that an uninhabited valley
branched off from Jokulsdale, and it seemed to him more
suitable for farming than any other valley he had ever
seen.

When Hrafnkel came back home, he asked his father to
divide up their property and said he wanted to start a farm
of his own. His father gave his approval, and Hrafnkel
built a home in that valley and called his farm Adalbol.
Hrafnkel married Oddbjorg Skjoldolf's daughter of Lax-
riverdale and they had two sons; the elder was called
Thorir and the younger Asbjorn.[2]

When Hrafnkel had settled at Adalbol, he had a large
temple built and held great sacrifices to the gods. He loved
Frey above all the other gods and gave him a half-share in
all his best treasures.

Hrafnkel took possession of the entire valley and gave
land to other settlers, on condition that he should be their
overlord. He became their priest and chieftain,[3] so he was

2. The opening of the story is freely based on the following passage in *Landnámabók* (Book of Settlements):
There was a man called Hrafnkel Hrafnsson who came to Iceland
towards the end of the Settlement Period [i.e. not long before 930].
He spent the first winter in Breiddale, but in the spring he travelled
north across the mountains. He took a rest in Skridudale and fell
asleep, and then he dreamed a man came to him and told him to
get up and leave at once. He woke up and set off, and he had only
gone a short distance when the mountain came crashing down and
killed a boar and a bull belonging to him. Afterwards he claimed
possession of Hrafnkelsdale and lived at Steinrodarstead. His sons
were Asbjorn, father of Helgi, and Thorir, father of the chieftain
Hrafnkel, father of Sveinbjorn.
3. According to *Landnámabók* Hrafnkel was one of the leading

given the nickname Frey's-Priest.[4] Hrafnkel was a bully despite his many qualities, and he forced the men of Jokulsdale to submit to his authority. He was kind and considerate to his own men, but harsh and ruthless to his enemies and to them he showed no justice. Hrafnkel fought many duels, but refused to pay compensation for the men he killed, and no one got any redress for the wrongs that Hrafnkel committed.

Fljotsdale Moor is stony and boggy and difficult to travel over, yet Hrafnkel and his father used to visit each other frequently, for they were on very affectionate terms. Hallfred thought the usual path across the moor was much too rough, so he looked for an alternative route south of the hills which rise on the moor, and there he found a drier but slightly longer way. This path has been called Hallfredargata ever since, and it can only be used by those who are thoroughly familiar with the moor.

3. FREYFAXI

A man called Bjarni lived at Laugarhouse in Hrafnkelsdale. He was married and had two sons by his wife, called

chieftains in the east of Iceland when the Althing was instituted in 930. At that time there were thirty-six priest-chieftains (*goðar*) in Iceland, but in 963 their number was increased to thirty-nine, and finally to forty-eight in the year 1005. These chieftains had various functions at the Althing and local Assemblies, acting as law-makers and nominating the judges for the courts. Their sacerdotal role came to an end with the introduction of Christianity in A.D. 1000.

4. *Freysgoði*. The god Frey seems to have been widely worshipped in pagan Iceland. The nickname Frey's-Priest is not associated with Hrafnkel in any other source, and it has been suggested that it may have been borrowed from Thord Frey's-Priest, the eponymous ancestor of the Freysgydlings, one of the leading families in Iceland during the 10th–13th centuries. For other saga references to Frey worshippers see e.g. *Vatnsdæla Saga* and *Killer-Glum's Saga*. In a late version of *Gisli's Saga* one of the protagonists is called Thorgrim Frey's-Priest.

Sam and Eyvind. They were handsome and likely fellows.
Eyvind stayed at home with his father, but Sam married
and settled down to farm at Leikskalar in the northern
part of the valley. Sam was a wealthy man; he was a skilled
lawyer and very conceited. Later Eyvind became a sea-
going trader and sailed to Norway where he stayed for one
winter. From there he travelled all the way to Constantinople where he lived for some time and enjoyed high
favours from the Byzantine Emperor.[5]

Hrafnkel had one treasured possession which he held
dearer than anything else he owned. It was a pale-dun stallion, with a black mane and a black stripe down the back.
He called the horse Freyfaxi and gave his patron Frey
a half-share in it. Hrafnkel loved this horse so passionately
that he swore a solemn oath to kill anyone who rode the
stallion without his permission.[6]

4. THE SHEPHERD

Bjarni had a brother called Thorbjorn who lived at Hol in
Hrafnkelsdale, on the east side of the river across from
Adalbol. Thorbjorn had slender means but a large family
to support. His eldest son was called Einar, a tall man and
very accomplished.

One spring Thorbjorn told Einar that he would have to
look elsewhere for work. 'The reason is, I can run the farm
with the help of my other children, and a man of your
ability should find it easy enough to get a job. It's not for

5. The sagas mention several Icelanders who were supposed to
have joined the Varangian Guard in Constantinople in the late 10th
or early 11th centuries. See e.g. *Grettir's Saga*, *Njal's Saga*, *Laxdæla
Saga*, *King Harald's Saga*, and *Halldor Snorrason* below.

6. The name *Freyfaxi* means literally 'Frey's black-maned stallion';
in *Vatnsdæla Saga* (ch. 34) there is a reference to a much-loved horse
bearing the same name. One version of *Olaf Tryggvason's Saga* mentions a herd of horses dedicated to Frey.

any lack of love that I'm sending you away, I love you more than my other children, but I've been driven to this by my poverty and lack of means. My other children are getting big enough for work now and you'll be able to get better employment than ever they could.'

Einar replied, 'You're rather late in telling me this, now all the best jobs have been taken by others. I don't like the idea of getting something no one else wants.'

One day Einar fetched his horse and rode over to Adalbol. Hrafnkel was sitting in the hall and gave him a friendly welcome. Einar asked Hrafnkel if he would hire him.

'Why are you so late in asking this?' said Hrafnkel. 'I'd rather have hired you than anyone else, but now I've already engaged servants for every job, except for one you couldn't possibly want.'

Einar asked him what he meant, and Hrafnkel said he'd not engaged a shepherd, although he needed one urgently. Einar replied he didn't mind what he did, whether it was this or something else. He also said he wanted to be hired for a whole year.

'I'll make you a quick offer,' said Hrafnkel. 'You're to herd fifty milch ewes at my shieling,[7] and gather in all the firewood for the summer as well. In return for this you can have your keep here for a whole year.

'There is one condition I must impose on you as I have on all my other shepherds. Freyfaxi grazes with his herd in the upper part of the valley, and you're to look after him in summer and winter. But I must warn you against one thing: I want you never to ride this horse, however

7. In Iceland, as in some other mountainous countries, it was customary to move the livestock to higher ground in the summer to make the best use of the grazing. The 'shieling' refers to the dairy and the sheds built to accommodate the herdsmen and dairymaids. See *Laxdæla Saga*, Penguin Classics, 1969, pp. 118, 186, 207.

urgent the need may seem to you, for I've sworn an oath to kill anyone who rides him. Some ten or twelve other horses go with Freyfaxi and you're free to use any of them, whenever you like, by day or night. Do as I tell you, for it's an old saying that "warning wards off blame". Now you know what I've sworn to do.'

Einar said that he would never be so wicked as to ride the one horse which was forbidden to him, particularly since there were plenty of other horses at his disposal.

5. TEMPTATION

Einar went home to fetch his clothes and came back to Adalbol to stay. Soon afterwards it was time to drive the ewes up to Grjotteigs Shieling in the upper reaches of Hrafnkelsdale. Einar was very good at his job and never lost a single sheep until about midsummer. Then some thirty sheep strayed one night, and Einar scoured all the pastures for them, but without success. The sheep were missing for nearly a week.

Early one morning Einar went outside and saw that the drizzle and mist had cleared up in the south. He took a staff, a bridle, and a saddle-cloth, and waded across Grjotteigs River which flows past the shieling. The sheep which had been there the night before were lying on the gravel flats down by the river. He drove them up to the shieling and set out in search of the missing ones. Then he noticed the horses farther down by the river and decided to catch one of them to ride on, for he kept thinking how much more ground he could cover by riding than by walking. But when he came closer, all the mares bolted away from him, and he chased them without success. They had never been so shy before. Only Freyfaxi remained behind; he was as still as if he were anchored to the ground.

Einar realized the morning was wearing on, and decided

to ride the stallion, thinking that Hrafnkel would never find out. So he bridled Freyfaxi, fixed the saddle-cloth on his back, and rode up along Grjotargill, south to the glacier and then west along the edge of the ice to the source of Jokuls River. From there he followed the river down to Reykja Shieling. He inquired at all the shielings whether any of the shepherds had seen his ewes, but no one had.

Einar rode Freyfaxi from dawn to mid-evening,[8] travelling fast and far, for this was an outstanding horse. Then it occurred to Einar that he had better drive in the sheep at the shieling, even though he had failed to find the others. So he rode east across the ridges over to Hrafnkelsdale, and when he came down to Grjotteig he heard the bleating of sheep beside the ravine which he had passed earlier in the morning. When he turned in that direction he saw thirty ewes come running towards him, and these were the sheep which had been missing for a week. He drove them in with the rest of the ewes. Then he led the stallion back to the herd and walked up to the shieling.

Freyfaxi was all running with sweat; and every hair on his body was dripping. He was covered in mud and panting with exhaustion. He rolled over a dozen times, and then neighed loudly and started to race down the path. Einar chased after him, hoping to catch him and bring him back to the mares, but the horse was so wild that Einar could not get anywhere near him.

Freyfaxi galloped down the valley without a pause, all the way to Adalbol. Hrafnkel was sitting at table. The horse came up to the door and neighed loudly. Hrafnkel told the woman who was serving at table to go to the door. 'A horse was neighing, and it sounded like Freyfaxi,' he said.

The woman went to the door and saw Freyfaxi standing

8. i.e. about 6 p.m.

outside in a filthy state. She told Hrafnkel that Freyfaxi
was there and looking very dirty.

'What could the champion want? Why has he come
home?' asked Hrafnkel. 'There can be no good reason for
this.'

He went outside, and when he saw Freyfaxi he said to
him, 'It grieves me to see how you have been treated, my
fosterling. You had your wits about when you came to
me, and this shall be avenged. Go back to your herd.'

The stallion left immediately and went up the valley to
his mares.

6. THE SHEPHERD'S DEATH

Hrafnkel went to bed that evening and slept soundly
through the night. In the morning he had a horse brought
in and saddled, and rode up to the shieling. He was wearing blue clothing and carrying an axe in his hand, and that
was the only weapon he had.

Einar had just driven the ewes into the fold and was
lying on the wall, counting them. The women were milking. They all greeted Hrafnkel, and he in turn asked how
Einar was getting on.

Einar replied, 'I've not been doing so well; thirty ewes
were lost for nearly a week, but now they've all been
found.'

Hrafnkel said he didn't mind about the sheep. 'But
hasn't something more serious happened? Why, the sheep
haven't strayed nearly as often as I'd have expected. Is it
true that you rode my Freyfaxi yesterday?'

Einar said he could not deny it.

Hrafnkel said, 'Why did you ride this one horse which
was forbidden to you, when there were plenty of other
horses you were free to ride? I'd have forgiven this single
offence if I'd not sworn so great an oath. You've made a

frank enough confession, but my faith tells me that nothing good can happen to people who break their solemn vows.'

Then he dismounted and killed Einar with a single blow.

Hrafnkel rode back home to Adalbol and told the news. He sent another man to the shieling to herd the sheep and had Einar's body buried on the hillock west of the shieling, where he raised a cairn over the grave. The cairn is called Einarsvarda, and the shieling people use it to mark the middle of the evening.

7. THE SHEPHERD'S FATHER

Thorbjorn of Hol heard how his son Einar had been killed, and he grieved at the news. He fetched his horse, rode over to Adalbol, and asked Hrafnkel for compensation for his son.

Hrafnkel replied that this was not the first man he had killed. 'Surely you must know I never pay compensation for anyone and people will have to put up with it. But I must admit this killing seems to me one of the worst acts I've ever committed.

'You have been my neighbour for a long time, and up till now I've liked you well, and you have also got on well with me. Einar and I would never have fallen out if he hadn't ridden the horse. How often we regret saying too much, and how seldom saying too little!

'I'm going to show how much worse I consider this killing than all the others I've done: I'll supply your household with plenty of milk in the summer and meat in the autumn, and I'll keep on doing this every year for as long as you choose to live on your farm. I'll also provide for your sons and daughters to give them a good start in life. And from now on you need only tell me if there's anything in my possession which you want and you'll have it and never have to do without. You can keep on farming for as long as you like, but move over here and stay with me when you tire of it, and I'll look after you for the rest of your life.

'This, then, must be a final settlement between us, and I'd expect everyone would agree with me that your son's been generously compensated for.'

'I will not accept this offer,' said Thorbjorn.

Hrafnkel asked, 'What do you want then?'

'I want us to choose arbitrators to settle the issue between us,' said Thorbjorn.

'Then you consider yourself my equal, and we can never be reconciled on those terms,' said Hrafnkel.

Thorbjorn went away and rode down the valley. He arrived at Laugarhouse and saw his brother Bjarni. Thorbjorn told him what had happened and asked him for help in the court action over Einar's killing.

Bjarni replied that he for one didn't consider himself to be Hrafnkel's equal. 'It's true that I'm a man of some property, but that doesn't mean I should take it on myself to quarrel with Hrafnkel, for it's a true enough saying that he's a wise man who knows himself. Hrafnkel has been known to crush wealthier opponents than me. In my opinion you've acted very stupidly, refusing his generous offer, and I'll have nothing to do with this.'

Thorbjorn had a good many harsh things to say to his brother and said the more people expected of him, the more his courage failed. With that he rode off, and so the brothers parted, hardly on the best of terms.

Thorbjorn rode on his way until he came to Leikskalar. He knocked on the door, and someone answered. Thorbjorn asked for Sam who came outside and gave his uncle a hearty welcome. When Sam invited Thorbjorn to stay he didn't answer and Sam realized that Thorbjorn was in an unhappy mood and asked him what had happened. Thorbjorn told him how Einar had been killed.

'It's nothing new that Hrafnkel's killing men,' said Sam. 'He's always been free with his axe.'

Thorbjorn asked Sam if he was willing to help him in any way. 'The fact of the matter is that although I'm the nearest of kin, the blow struck not so far from yourself.'

'Have you asked for any compensation from Hrafnkel?' asked Sam.

Thorbjorn told him precisely what had happened between Hrafnkel and himself.

'I've never known Hrafnkel to make such an offer before,' said Sam. 'I'll ride with you up to Adalbol; we must approach Hrafnkel humbly and ask him if his original offer still holds. He'll certainly be generous in one way or another.'

'There are two objections,' said Thorbjorn. 'Hrafnkel will no longer be willing and the arrangement is no more agreeable to me now than it was when I left him.'

Sam said, 'In my opinion Hrafnkel's going to be a hard man to oppose in a court action.'

Thorbjorn replied, 'The reason why you young men get nowhere is that you overestimate the obstacles every time. I don't believe anyone could have such wretches for kinsmen as I have. I think men like you are despicable; you consider yourself a good lawyer and are keen on petty lawsuits, but you refuse to take on this case, urgent though it is. You'll come in for a great deal of criticism over this, and not without reason, for you're the most conceited of all of our kin. I can see now what the outcome of my case is likely to be.'

'In what way will it benefit you, if I take over this action and the two of us are humiliated?' said Sam.

'It would mean a great deal to me if you were to take this case,' said Thorbjorn, 'no matter what comes of it.'

'I'm very reluctant to bring an action against Hrafnkel,' said Sam. 'I'll do so only because we're kinsmen, but I want you to know that in my opinion I'm helping a fool in helping you.'

Sam held out his hand and formally took over the action from Thorbjorn.

8. THE LAWYER

Sam had a horse brought in and rode up the valley to a certain farm, and there he gave notice of the charge against Hrafnkel for the killing. Hrafnkel heard about this and thought it amusing that Sam had started proceedings against him.

The summer passed, and the following winter. In the spring at summons days[9] Sam rode from home up to Adalbol and served a summons on Hrafnkel for the killing of Einar. Then Sam rode down the valley and cited the neighbours who would ride to the Althing with him, and after that he stayed quietly at home until it was time to get ready for the Althing.[10]

Hrafnkel sent men down to Jokulsdale to gather forces, and altogether he got seventy men from his district. With this force he rode east across Fljotsdale Moor, then round the head of the lake and across the ridge over to Skridu-dale, up through that valley, south over Oxar Moor to Berufjord, and from there he followed the usual route to Sida. The journey from Fljotsdale to Thingvellir takes seventeen days.

When Hrafnkel had left the district Sam gathered forces, and the neighbours he had already cited were the

9. The last day for serving an Althing summons was four weeks before the Althing convened. See *Njal's Saga*, Penguin Classics, 1960, p. 127n.

10. In the tenth century the Althing used to meet on the ninth Thursday of summer, about the middle of June.

only farmers to accompany him; and the rest were vag
rants. He supplied these men with weapons, clothes and
food. Sam took a different route out of the valley. He rode
north to the bridge and crossed the river there, then over
Modrudale Moor and spent the night at Modrudale. From
there they rode to Herdibreidstongue, and then down by
Blafell and over to Kroksdale, and so south to Sand near
Sandafell and then to Thingvellir. When they came there,
Hrafnkel had not yet arrived. Sam furnished a booth[11] for
his men far from the place where the Eastfjords people
usually stay.

Shortly afterwards Hrafnkel arrived at the Althing. He
fitted out his booth as usual, and when he heard that Sam
was also present at the Althing he thought it vastly amusing.

The Althing was well attended. Most of the chieftains
in the land were present. Sam went to every one of them
for their help and support, but they all gave the same
answer: that they did not stand in such debt to Sam that
they were willing to get involved in a quarrel with Hrafnkel the Priest and so risk their reputations. They argued
that those who had brought actions against Hrafnkel at
previous assemblies had all suffered the same humiliation,
for Hrafnkel had got the better of it in every single law-
suit which had been brought against him.

Sam went back to his booth. He and Thorbjorn were dis-
heartened and feared they would not only lose their case
but also be ashamed and humiliated because of it. They
were in such a state they could neither eat nor sleep. All
the chieftains refused to help them, even those they had
expected to give them support.

11. The 'booths' at the Althing which are so often referred to in
the sagas were temporary shelters. They had permanent walls of turf
and stone, but the roof and other furnishings were put up every year
for the duration of the Althing only.

9. THE BENEFACTOR

Early one morning old Thorbjorn woke up. He roused Sam and asked him to get up. 'I can't sleep,' he said.

Sam got up and dressed. They went outside and down to Oxar River below the bridge, and there they washed themselves.

Thorbjorn said to Sam, 'My advice is that we have our horses brought and get ready to ride back home, for it's obvious that humiliation is all we can expect here.'

Sam answered, 'That's very interesting, for it was you who insisted on bringing this lawsuit against Hrafnkel and refused an offer which would have satisfied any other man taking action over the killing of a kinsman. You questioned the courage of all of us who were reluctant to help you with this lawsuit. That's the reason why I'll never give up until it's utterly past hope that I could achieve anything at all.'

When Sam had spoken these words Thorbjorn was so moved that he wept.

Then they noticed a group of five men walking from a certain booth on the west bank of the river, some distance farther down. The man in the lead was tall, but not strongly built; he was wearing a leaf-green tunic and carrying an ornamented sword in his hand; he had regular features and a ruddy face, and there was an air of distinction about him; he had a fine head of hair, and was easily recognized because of a light lock on the left side.

'We must get moving,' said Sam, 'and go west across the river to meet these people.'

They walked down by the river, and this man in the lead was the first to greet them and ask who they were. They told him, and Sam asked him his name. He said he was called Thorkel Thjostarsson. Sam also asked him about his home and background, and Thorkel replied that he belonged to the Westfjords by family and origin and that his home was in Thorskafjord.

'Are you a chieftain?' asked Sam.

He said far from it.

'Are you a farmer then?' said Sam.

He said he was not.

'What kind of a man are you then?' said Sam.

'I'm a wanderer,' he replied. 'I returned from abroad the year before last, after I'd been away from Iceland for six years and travelled south to Constantinople where I was in service with the Emperor of Byzantium. But now I'm staying with my brother Thorgeir.'

'Is he a chieftain?' said Sam.

'He certainly is,' said Thorkel. 'His authority extends over Thorskafjord and some parts of the Westfjords as well.'

'Is he present at the Althing?' said Sam.

'Yes, he is.'

'How many men has he got with him?'

'Seventy,' said Thorkel.

'Are there more of you brothers?' said Sam.

'There's a third brother,' said Thorkel.

'Who is he?' asked Sam.

'His name's Thormod,' said Thorkel, 'and he lives at Gardar in Alptaness. He is married to Thordis, the daughter of Thorolf Skallagrimsson of Borg.'[12]

'Will you give us some help?' said Sam.

'What do you want?' asked Thorkel.

'The help and support of chieftains,' said Sam, 'for we're bringing a lawsuit against Hrafnkel the Priest for killing Einar Thorbjarnarson. We can depend on my pleading all right as long as we have the benefit of your support.'

12. Thorolf was the brother of Egil Skallagrimsson, the eponymous hero of *Egil's Saga*. His daughter Thordis is known from other sources, and was not the wife of Thormod Thjostarsson.

'I've already told you that I'm no chieftain,' said Thorkel.

'Why were you disinherited?' said Sam. 'You're a chieftain's son just like your brothers.'

'I never said I didn't hold the chieftaincy,' said Thorkel. 'But I handed over my share in it to my brother Thorgeir before I went abroad. I've not resumed my authority since, for I consider it in good hands as long as he's in charge of it. You'd better go and see Thorgeir and ask for his support. He's a man of the highest principles, brave and capable in everything he does, and young and ambitious too. He's the kind of man most likely to give you real support.'

'We'll never get anything from him,' said Sam, 'unless you plead with him on our behalf.'

'I promise to be for you rather than against,' said Thorkel, 'for it seems to me that to take legal action over the killing of a close kinsman is a very urgent matter indeed.

'Go across into his booth right away. The people there are still asleep. You'll see two hammocks near the inner gable of the booth; I sleep in one of them, and my brother Thorgeir has the other. He's had a great boil on his foot since he came to the Althing, so he's slept little at night, but early this morning the boil burst and the core's out. He's been sleeping since, and now he's stretched his foot from under the bedclothes and on to the foot-board, to ease the inflammation in the foot.

'The old man had better go into the booth first and in along the floor – he looks half-blind and decrepit to me. When you, old man, come up to the hammock you're to stumble heavily and fall on to the foot-board, catch hold of the bandaged toe and jerk it towards you. We'll see how Thorgeir responds to this treatment.'

'You probably mean well,' said Sam, 'but this doesn't seem wise to me.'

Thorkel answered, 'Either do as I tell you, or go to someone else for advice.'

'We'd better do as he tells us,' said Sam.

Thorkel told them he would be coming along later. 'I'm waiting for my men,' he said.

10. THE BROTHERS

Sam and Thorbjorn walked over to the booth and went in. All the men inside were still asleep, and they could see where Thorgeir was lying. The old man was in the lead, stumbling heavily, and when he came to the hammock he fell across the foot-board, snatched at the ailing toe and pulled it hard towards him. Thorgeir woke up with a start, jumped out of the hammock and asked who these clumsy people were, trampling on the feet of the sick. Sam and Thorbjorn could think of nothing to say.

Then Thorkel stepped into the booth and said to his brother Thorgeir, 'Don't be so quick to lose your temper over this, kinsman, for you'll come to no harm. People's actions are often worse than their intentions, and they find it particularly difficult to pay full attention to everything when they have a lot on their minds. Your excuse, kinsman, is that your foot is tender and it's given you a lot of trouble. That's a pain only you can feel. It could be that an old man won't feel any less suffering over the death of his son, particularly since he has no means of redress and is completely helpless. That's a pain only he can feel. It stands to reason that a man with so much on his mind can't be expected to pay full attention to things.'

'I don't see why he should put the blame on me,' said Thorgeir. 'I didn't kill his son, so there's no need for him to take it out on me.'

'He didn't mean to take it out on you,' said Thorkel, 'but he came at you harder than he intended and for that

51

you can only blame his feeble eyesight. He was hoping that you would help him, and really, it would be a noble gesture to aid this poor old man, for it's necessity and not greed that makes him take legal action over the killing of his son. All the chieftains have refused to help these men, which only shows how small-minded they really are.'

'Whom are these men accusing?' said Thorgeir.

'Hrafnkel the Priest has killed Thorbjorn's son for no reason,' said Thorkel. 'He commits one crime after another and, whatever he does, he refuses to pay any compensation.'

Thorgeir answered, 'I shall do exactly the same as the other chieftains, for I don't think I'm in any sense indebted to these men so that I'd want to start an argument with Hrafnkel. Every summer he seems to give the same treatment to anyone who tries to prosecute him: they always finish up without the least satisfaction to their honour. I've seen this happen to every one of them. That's why most people aren't keen to get involved in a lawsuit against Hrafnkel, unless they're driven to it by sheer necessity.'

'If I were a chieftain I might behave exactly like the other chiefs and find it just as hard to fight with Hrafnkel,' said Thorkel. 'But I don't think so, because the man who'd beaten every previous opponent is the one I'd like most as my adversary. In my opinion it would be greatly to the credit of any chieftain if somehow or other he could restrain Hrafnkel, and even if I failed like everyone else before me I shouldn't feel humbled, I could accept what has happened to so many others – nothing ventured, nothing gained.'

'Now I can see what you have in mind,' said Thorgeir. 'You want me to help these men. I'm going to hand our chieftaincy and authority over to you, and then you'll be in charge for the same time as I've held it already. Afterwards we can share it equally between us, but meanwhile you can help anyone you want.'

'I think it would be in our best interest if you were to manage our chieftaincy for a long time to come,' said Thorkel. 'I'd like you rather than anyone else to be in charge of it, for in many respects you're the ablest of us brothers. As for myself, I've not quite made up my mind what I'll be doing in the near future. As you know, kinsman, I've not meddled in many affairs since I came back to Iceland. I can see now how much my advice is appreciated, so I'm not going to press the matter any further for the time being. But it's quite possible that Thorkel Lock[13] may go somewhere else, where his word will carry more weight than it does here.'

Thorgeir said, 'Now I can see what the matter is, kinsman. You're offended, and I can't stand the thought of that; so we'd better help these men just as you wish, whatever comes of it.'

'I only want you to know,' said Thorkel, 'that it will please me if you do me this favour.'

'What do these men think they can achieve?' said Thorgeir. 'What contribution can they make to the success of their lawsuit?'

'As I was saying earlier this morning,' said Sam, 'we need the backing of chieftains; but I can conduct the actual pleading myself.'

Thorgeir said in that case it would be easy to help him. 'And now, it's important to prepare the case as well as possible,' he said. 'I think Thorkel would like you to come and see him before the court convenes. You'll then reap something from your stubbornness, one way or the other, either some comfort or else even greater humiliation, disappointment and disgrace. Go back to your booth now and keep cheerful for you'll need to show some confidence if

13. The nickname refers to the lock of his hair, see Ch. 9.

you're to stand up against Hrafnkel. But don't tell anyone about our promise to help you.'

When Sam and Thorbjorn came back to their own booth they were feeling happy. Their followers were surprised to see how suddenly their mood had changed for they'd been in low spirits when they'd left.

11. HRAFNKEL'S HUMILIATION

They waited quietly till the court convened, and then Sam called on his men to go with him to the Law Rock. The court was sitting and Sam went boldly before the judges, named his witnesses at once and pleaded his case against Hrafnkel the Priest in full accordance with the laws of the land. He did so forcefully and without any flaws in procedure. Then the Thjostarssons came up with a large following. All the farmers from the West supported them, and it was obvious that the Thjostarssons had a great number of friends. Sam conducted his case to the point where Hrafnkel was invited to present his defence. Anyone else in court who was willing and competent to defend him legally could have done so on his behalf. There was a loud applause at Sam's speech, but no one present was willing to take over the defence on Hrafnkel's part.

Some people rushed over to Hrafnkel's booth to tell him what had happened. He wasted no time, called on his men and went to the court, not expecting to meet with any opposition. He was determined to discourage men of little account from bringing lawsuits against him, for he intended to break up the court by force and so put an end to Sam's action. But there was no chance of that now, because a large number of people had gathered there and Hrafnkel could get nowhere near the court. He was barred from approaching it by sheer weight of numbers, so he couldn't even hear what the prosecutor was saying and it was impossible for him to present his legal defence. Sam followed up his case demanding the maximum penalty, and so it came about that Hrafnkel was sentenced to full outlawry then and there at the Althing.

Hrafnkel went back to his booth, had his horses brought in and rode away from the Althing. He was very annoyed at the outcome of the case, for nothing like this had ever happened to him before. He rode east across Lyngdale Moor, from there east to Sida, and didn't stop until he reached home again at Adalbol in Hrafnkelsdale. He stayed at home as if nothing had happened.

Sam remained behind at the Althing and went about with a swagger. Many people were delighted that Hrafnkel had been so humiliated for they called to mind all the injustice he had shown to others on previous occasions.

12. THE NEXT MOVE

Sam waited until the Althing was dissolved and people were ready to go home. He thanked the brothers for their help. Thorgeir laughed and asked him what he thought of the outcome, and Sam replied he was very pleased.

'Do you really think you're any better off now than you were before?' asked Thorgeir.

'In my opinion Hrafnkel has suffered great humiliation and it will long be remembered,' said Sam. 'And then there's a good deal of money involved too.'

'The man isn't a full outlaw until the court of confiscation has been held, and that must be done at his legal domicile, fourteen days after the *weapontake*.' (*Weapontake* is when people ride home from the Althing.)[14]

14. The saga's definition of the legal term *weapontake* (*vápnatak*) agrees with early Icelandic usage. It refers to the custom that everyone had to lay his weapons aside while the Althing was in session and was only allowed to resume them when it broke up.

'I suppose Hrafnkel will be back home by now,' Thorgeir went on, 'and that he'll be intending to remain at Adalbol. I think he'll keep his chieftaincy too, in spite of you. But you'll be meaning to ride back home and at best stay there – if you're lucky enough. I suppose you'll gain this much from your lawsuit that you can now call him "your outlaw", but he'll no doubt carry on bullying everyone just as he always did, and the only difference will be that you'll now have to grovel lower than ever.'

'That doesn't bother me in the least,' said Sam.

'You're a brave man!' said Thorgeir. 'But I don't think my brother Thorkel is going to leave you in the lurch. He means to give you all the help he can until you've settled your business with Hrafnkel once and for all, and then you can live in peace. It's our obvious duty to keep on supporting you to the hilt since we're already so much involved, so we're going with you to the Eastfjords. Do you know of any route to the east that's not commonly used?'

Sam said he'd follow the same route back that he had taken from the east, and he was very pleased with the offer.

13. TORTURE

Thorgeir picked out forty men to go with them, and Sam had another forty, all of them well equipped with weapons and horses. They went off following the same route as before, and reached Jokulsdale at dawn on the day the court of confiscation was due to take place. Then they crossed the river by bridge.

Thorgeir asked how they could best take Hrafnkel by surprise, and Sam said he knew the answer to that. He turned sharply away from the path and up the mountainside and then along the ridge between Hrafnkelsdale and Jokulsdale until they reached the mountain above the farm at Adalbol. There were grassy hollows stretching up to the moor there and the hillside sloped steeply down to the farm in the valley below.

Sam dismounted and said, 'If you take my advice, we'll all get off here. We'll leave the horses behind, with twenty men to watch them, and the remaining sixty will make a rush down to the farm. The slope's so steep we'll be quicker without the horses. I don't expect many people at Adalbol will be up at this hour.'

They did as Sam suggested; this place has been known as Hrossageilar[15] ever since. They set off running and raced down so fast that they reached the farmstead just after rising time[16] but the people hadn't got up yet. They rammed the door with a log and charged into the house.

Hrafnkel was still in bed. They seized him and all the other able-bodied men and took them outside. The women and children were herded into one room. In the home meadow there stood a store-house and between it and the wall of the farmhouse there was a beam for drying clothes. They led Hrafnkel up to the beam. He kept pleading for himself and his men, and when he realized that all his efforts were in vain, he asked the lives of his men be spared.

'They've done you no harm,' he said, 'but you can kill me without any discredit to yourselves. I'm not going to plead for my life, but I ask you not to torture me, for that would bring you no credit.'

Thorkel said, 'We've heard about how little mercy you've shown to your own opponents, and it's only fair you should be made to feel the pain now.'

Then they got hold of Hrafnkel and his men and tied their hands behind their backs. After that they broke open the store-house and took some ropes down off the pegs. Then they drew their knives, cut through the prisoners'

15. Literally 'Horse-lanes'.
16. i.e. about 6 a.m.

heels behind the tendon, pulled the rope through the holes, strung the eight men together and hung them from the clothes' beam.

'You're getting just what you deserve, Hrafnkel,' said Thorgeir. 'You must have thought it very unlikely you'd ever be so humiliated by anyone as you are now. Which do you prefer, Thorkel: to stay here and keep an eye on Hrafnkel and his men, or go with Sam an arrow-shot from the farmstead and hold the court of confiscation on a stony mound, away from fields and meadows?'

(This had to be done with the sun due south.)

'I'll stay here with Hrafnkel,' said Thorkel, 'It seems to me the easier job of the two.'

Thorgeir and Sam went off and held the court of confiscation. Afterwards they came back to the farmhouse, took Hrafnkel and his men down and laid them on the ground. Their eyes were all bloodshot.

Thorgeir said to Sam that he could do what he liked with Hrafnkel. 'I think he's manageable now,' he added. 'It's easy to see Hrafnkel never expected to find himself in your hands.'

'I'm giving Hrafnkel a choice of two things,' said Sam. 'One, that he'll be taken to a place I'll choose and be put to death there. But since he has so many dependents in his care I'm willing to give him the chance of looking after them. If he wants me to spare his life he's to leave Adalbol with his entire household and take away with him only such goods as I let him, which will be very little indeed. I'll take away your authority and estate, Hrafnkel. You and your heirs are never to claim these back, and you're never to settle on this side of Fljotsdale Moor. If you are willing to accept these terms, shake hands on them now.'

'Most people would prefer a quick death to such a humiliation,' said Hrafnkel, 'but I'll do as many others have done and choose life as long as I have the chance. I'm doing this mostly for the sake of my sons, for they'll have little hope of success if I die now.'

When Hrafnkel had agreed to Sam's terms, he was set free and Sam doled out to him what he saw fit, which was very little indeed. On that very day Hrafnkel moved out of Adalbol with his entire family and the few belongings he was allowed to take.

Thorkel said to Sam, 'I can't understand why you're doing this. You'll have good reason to regret you've spared Hrafnkel's life.'

Sam said that was the way it was going to be.

14. NEW LIFE

Hrafnkel travelled east across Fljotsdale Moor and over to the far side of Fljotsdale, east of Lagarwater. There was a little farm called Lokhilla at the head of the lake, and he bought it on credit, as all he had were some provisions for his household.

There was a great deal of talk about this, how his arrogance had been deflated, and many people called to mind the old saying that 'Short is the life of the proud'.

The land that Hrafnkel bought was extensive and heavily wooded, but the farm buildings were poor, which was the reason he could buy it at such a low price. But Hrafnkel spared no expense: he felled a lot of timber, for there was plenty of it, and built a fine house. The place has been known as Hrafnkelsstead ever since and is still considered a good farm.

Hrafnkel lived the first year there in great hardship, but he improved his resources by sending his men fishing. Hrafnkel himself worked very hard while he was building the house. He raised every calf and every kid the first year, and he was so successful with his livestock that hardly any of his beasts failed; in fact they were so productive they gave him almost double the normal yield. That summer Lagarwater was teeming with trout, which proved very profitable for the farmers in the district, and this continued for a good many years.

15. FREYFAXI'S DEATH

A little after Sam had taken over the farm at Adalbol from Hrafnkel, he held a magnificent feast to which he invited all the farmers who had been Hrafnkel's supporters and offered to be their chieftain in his place. They accepted this but some of them had misgivings about it.

The Thjostarssons advised him to be kind, generous and helpful to his men and to support them in anything they needed.

'They would be worthless men if they failed to give you loyal support then, whenever you needed it. We're giving you this advice because we want you to succeed in everything and we think you're really a very brave man. Be careful now and stay on your guard, one must always watch out for the wicked.'

Later that day the Thjostarssons had Freyfaxi and his herd sent for and said they wanted to see these animals about which there'd been so much talk, as they were supposed to be exceptionally fine horses. The horses were brought in and the brothers looked them over.

'I think these mares could be of some help on the farm,' said Thorgeir, 'and it is my advice that they should be put to some useful work until they're too old to live. But the stallion doesn't seem better than any other horse, rather worse in fact, since he's been the cause of so much trouble. I don't want any more killings to be caused by him than have taken place already, and it's only proper that his present owner should have him.'

They led the stallion across the meadow and then down

along the river. Below the farmstead there are high cliffs
and a waterfall with a deep pool underneath. They led
the stallion on to the bluff. Then the Thjostarssons pulled
a bag over Freyfaxi's head, tied long heavy poles to his
flanks, fastened a stone to his neck, and with the poles they
pushed the horse over the cliff. So the horse perished, and
the bluff has been known as Freyfaxahamar ever since.

Down there stood Hrafnkel's temple, and Thorgeir decided to burn it. He had all the gods stripped, set fire to
the temple and burnt everything to ashes.

Then they went back to the farm. The guests got ready
to leave, and Sam chose fine gifts for everyone. The
brothers also made arrangements for their departure, and
Sam gave them splendid gifts. They exchanged firm vows
of friendship and parted on affectionate terms. The
brothers rode the shortest way to the Westfjords and came
back home to Thorskafjord with their reputation greatly
enhanced.

Sam placed Thorbjorn at Leikskalar and told him to
farm there. Sam's wife joined him at Adalbol, and he lived
there for some time.

16. HRAFNKEL'S NEW CHIEFTAINCY

East in Fljotsdale, Hrafnkel heard what the Thjostarssons
had done, the killing of his Freyfaxi and the burning of
the gods and the temple in Hrafnkelsdale.

Then Hrafnkel said, 'I think it's a vain thing to believe
in the gods.' He declared he wouldn't worship them any
longer, and he kept his vow, for he never held any sacrifices again.

Hrafnkel lived at Hrafnkelsstead and got very rich. He
soon gained a position of power in the district, and everyone was eager to stand or sit, just as Hrafnkel wished. In
those days there were regular sailings from Norway to Ice-

land, and most of the district was settled in Hrafnkel's time. No one was allowed to live there without Hrafnkel's leave and every farmer had to promise him his support; in return Hrafnkel gave them his protection. He gained authority over all the districts east of Lagarwater, so his new chieftaincy soon became much larger in area and contained a greater number of people than the one he had controlled before, for it reached as far north as Selwater and south into Skridudale, covering the entire Lagarwater region.

Hrafnkel was a changed man now, and much better liked than he used to be. He could still be as helpful and generous as before, but he'd become gentler and quieter in every way.

Sam and Hrafnkel often met at assemblies, but they never spoke about their dealings. Sam enjoyed his high position for six years. He was well liked by his supporters, for he didn't forget the advice the brothers had given him and was quiet and gentle and ready to solve everyone's problems.

17. THE TRAVELLER

One summer a ship put in at Reydarfjord; its captain was Eyvind Bjarnason. He had been abroad for seven years and had greatly improved himself and now he was a highly successful man. He was soon told what had happened, but he didn't say much about it, being a man who never meddled in other people's affairs.

When Sam heard of his brother's arrival he rode to the ship, and there was a happy reunion between them. Sam invited Eyvind to come west and stay with him and he accepted readily but asked Sam first to ride home and send him horses for the luggage. Then Eyvind had his ship hauled ashore and saw to the cargo, while Sam did as his brother suggested, went home, had some horses brought in and sent servants with them to fetch Eyvind. When Eyvind had seen to his cargo, he loaded the pack-horses and made ready to ride west to Hrafnkelsdale, travelling up along Reydarfjord.

There were five men riding together; the sixth was Eyvind's servant-boy, who was an Icelander and closely related to Eyvind and Sam. Eyvind had saved this boy from utter poverty before he left Iceland, had taken him abroad and treated him just like himself. This noble gesture brought Eyvind a great deal of credit, and everyone agreed that there were few men like him.

They rode up to Thordale Moor and drove sixteen pack-horses before them. Two of the men were Sam's servants, and the remaining four were travellers. These wore coloured clothing and carried bright shields. They rode across Skridudale and then over the ridge into Fljotsdale through Bulungavellir, and down to Gilsareyr which lies to the east of the lake between Hallormsstead and Hrafnkelsstead. Then they continued their ride up along Lagarwater, below the home meadow at Hrafnkelsstead, round the head of the lake, and crossed Jokuls River at Skala Ford. It was then half-way between rising time and midmorning.

Down by the lake a servant was washing her clothes, and when she saw the riders she bundled together the linen and ran up to the farm. She threw the laundry down beside the log-pile outside the door and burst into the room. Hrafnkel had not yet got up, and some of his most trusted men were resting in the hall, but all the farmhands had gone to work. This was the haymaking season.

The woman started talking as soon as she came in. 'The old saying is true enough, "The older a man, the feebler." The honour a man's given early in life isn't worth much, if he has to give it all up in disgrace, and hasn't the courage to fight for his rights ever again. It's a peculiar thing indeed to happen to those who were once thought brave. As for those who grew up with their father and who seemed to you utterly worthless compared to yourself, it's a different story, for as soon as they reached manhood they went abroad, travelling from country to country, and when they come back they're thought very highly of, even above chieftains. Eyvind Bjarnason was just crossing the river at Skala Ford carrying a bright shield that shone in the sun. He's a worthy target for revenge, an outstanding man like him.'

The woman kept on gabbling.

Hrafnkel got to his feet and spoke to her. 'There's probably a lot of truth in what you're saying, but your motives hardly do you credit, so you deserve some extra trouble. Hurry over to Vidivellir and ask the sons of Hallstein, Sighvat and Snorri, to come here as quickly as they can with all their able-bodied men.'

Hrafnkel sent another woman out to Hrolfsstead for Thord and Halli, the sons of Hrolf, and other able-bodied men there, all brave and capable men. Hrafnkel also sent for his own farmhands and including them there were eighteen men altogether. They armed themselves resolutely, and rode across the river where the others had forded before.

18. THE TRAVELLER'S DEATH

When Hrafnkel was riding across the valley, Eyvind and his men had already reached the moor and they continued their ride till they came west of the middle of the moor, to a place called Bersagotur. There is a swamp there, and one has to ride through watery slush, with the mud reaching up to the horse's knee or mid-leg, sometimes even up to its belly; but underneath the mud the rock is very firm so there's no risk of sinking any deeper. West of this bog the

terrain is very stony, and Eyvind and his men rode on to
it.

When they came to the rocky ground, the boy looked
back and said to Eyvind, 'There are some men riding after
us, eighteen or twenty of them. One of the riders is a tall
man in blue and he seems to me very like Hrafnkel,
though I've not set eyes on him for quite a long time.'

'What's that to do with us?' said Eyvind. 'As far as I
know I've nothing to fear from Hrafnkel's movements, for
I've never done him any harm. He must be on his way to
the valley to see his friends there.'

'I have a feeling it's you he wants to see,' said the boy.

'I'm not aware there's been any clash between him and
my brother Sam since they made their agreement,' said
Eyvind.

The boy said, 'I'd like you to ride ahead west to the valley; then you'll be safe. I know Hrafnkel's temper well
enough to be certain we've nothing to fear from him
should he fail to get you. All's well as long as you're kept
out of danger, for there's nothing to tempt them then.
Whatever happens, we'll come to no harm.'

Eyvind said he wasn't going to ride away. 'I'm not even
sure who these men are, and I'd be the laughing-stock of
everyone if I ran off without further proof.'

They rode on west across the rocky ground, and then
they came to another swamp which is called Oxmire. It's
very grassy and has a good many soft patches which make
it almost impassable. This bog is about as wide as the previous one but much softer, so that travellers have to dismount. That is why old Hallfred used to take the upper
path, even though it was longer; in his opinion these two
swamps were almost total barriers.

Eyvind and his men rode west into the swamp, and they
were so often bogged down they were very much delayed.
The pursuers, with no pack-horses to slow them down,

were travelling much faster. When Hrafnkel and his men rode into the bog, the others were just clear of it. Eyvind and his men could now clearly recognize Hrafnkel and his two sons among the pursuers, and many others besides.

Eyvind's companions urged him to ride away. 'All the obstacles are behind us now, and it's an easy ride west from the moor. You can reach Adalbol while they're tackling the swamp, and once you're there you're safe.'

Eyvind said, 'I'm not going to run away from someone I've never wronged.'

They rode west from the swamp and up the ridge. West of the ridge there's a fine grassy valley, and west of the valley another ridge, and west of the second ridge lies Hrafnkelsdale. They rode up the easternmost ridge. There are some humps on the ridge, and on the slope stands a steep knoll, with lyme grass on top but eroded by the wind on all sides. This is fine land for grazing, but near it lies a bog. Eyvind rode away from the path and into the hollow east of the lyme knoll. He dismounted and told his companions to let their horses graze there for a while.

'Now we'll soon find out what our lot is to be,' he said, 'and whether these men will turn on us or go about their business west to the valley.'

By this time, Hrafnkel and his men had almost caught up with them. Eyvind hobbled his horse, and went up on to the knoll with his companions; then they tore up some stones from the sides of the knoll. Hrafnkel turned from the path and south to the knoll, and without a single word to Eyvind he attacked them at once. Eyvind defended himself with courage and determination.

Eyvind's servant thought he wasn't strong enough to fight, so he took his horse, rode west across the ridge over to Adalbol, and told Sam what was happening. Sam wasted no time and sent for help to the neighbouring farms. He got twenty men, all of them well equipped, and with these he rode east to the moor where the encounter had taken place. When he arrived on the scene it was all over. Hrafnkel was riding east across the moor having completed his mission and Eyvind and all his men lay there dead. The first thing Sam did was to see whether there was any sign of life in his brother, but the killers had done their work thoroughly. They were all dead; twelve of Hrafnkel's men were dead too, but six of them had got away.

Sam wasted no time there, but told his men to ride after them at once. 'They have tired horses, but ours are all fresh, and maybe we'll just be able to catch up with them before they get away from the moor.'

By this time Hrafnkel had already cleared Oxmire, and the chase was on. When Sam and his men had passed through the bog and come to the rocky part, Hrafnkel had just crossed it, so this was the only obstacle between them. While Sam was tackling the rocks, Hrafnkel widened the distance between them, but Sam and his men rode on till they reached the edge of the moor and saw Hrafnkel far away down the hill-side. Sam realized then that Hrafnkel would get away down to the farms.

Sam told his men not to ride any farther. 'We must turn back, because Hrafnkel will find it easy to gather forces, and then we'd be completely in his power.'

So Sam turned back and came to the place where Eyvind lay dead. He set to work and raised a burial mound over him and his dead companions. The places there are called Eyvindartorfa, Eyvindarfell, and Eyvindardale.

19. SAM'S HUMILIATION

Sam told his men to round up Eyvind's horses, and then they loaded the pack-horses and drove them down to Adalbol. As soon as he got back home Sam sent for forces throughout Hrafnkelsdale, asking all his supporters to be there early in the morning, for he intended to ride east across the moor.

'We'll see how our trip goes,' he said.

When Sam went to bed in the evening, a number of men had already gathered at Adalbol.

Hrafnkel rode back home to Hrafnkelsstead that evening and told the news. After he had had a meal he gathered forces and got together seventy men. With this force he rode west across the moor, came unexpectedly to Adalbol, caught Sam in bed, and gave him a choice of two alternatives.

'Now, Sam, you find yourself in a position which can't have seemed likely to you some time ago,' said Hrafnkel. 'Your life's in my hands. I'll be just as generous to you as you were to me, and give you the same choice: to live or to be killed. If you choose to live, the terms will be solely up to me.'

Sam said he'd prefer to live, though either alternative would be harsh.

Hrafnkel told him he could be certain of that, 'for I owe you nothing less. I'd have treated you much better if you'd deserved it. You're to leave Adalbol, move down to Leikskalar and settle there on your farm. You can take away with you all the goods Eyvind brought with him, but you'll not be allowed to take anything else away from here, unless people are willing to testify you brought it with you to Adalbol. Such belongings you may carry off with you. I'll resume my authority and chieftaincy over this district, and take over the estate with all the other possessions that used to be mine. I can see there's been a vast increase in my wealth, but you won't benefit from it, as I'll be taking it all for myself. You'll get no compensation for your brother Eyvind, because of the cruel revenge you took for the killing of your other kinsman, and you've had more than enough compensation for your cousin Einar while you've been enjoying my power and wealth all this time. I don't believe the killing of Eyvind was any worse than the torture I was made to suffer, nor was the death of his companions any worse than the maiming of my men. You had me outlawed from my own district, but I'll allow you to live at Leikskalar as long as you don't let your pride be your downfall. You'll be my subordinate for the rest of our lives, and you can be sure your position will be lower than it's ever been.'

Then Sam moved over to Leikskalar with his family and settled down on his farm.

20. APPEAL FOR HELP

Hrafnkel took over the farm at Adalbol and brought his household there; it was a prosperous and well-stocked farm. He left his son Thorir in charge at Hrafnkelsstead, with a housekeeper to help him. Hrafnkel now held authority over many districts. His son Asbjorn came to Adalbol to stay with his father, since he was the younger.

Sam stayed that winter at Leikskalar. He was taciturn and kept very much to himself, and it was obvious to everyone that he was unhappy with the way things were going. Late in the winter when the days grew longer, Sam had his horses shod and hired a groom to accompany him on a journey. They had three horses, one of them carrying Sam's clothes. They rode over the bridge and then across Modrudale Moor and forded Jokuls River up in the mountains. Then they rode on to Mywater, and from there across Fljots Moor and Ljosawater Pass; they kept going without a halt until they reached Thorskafjord. Sam was given a good welcome there. Thorkel had just arrived from abroad where he'd been for four years.

Sam stayed there for a week enjoying the rest. Then he

told the brothers about his dealings with Hrafnkel and asked them for help and support as before.

On this occasion it was Thorgeir who spoke on behalf of the brothers. He said they were very unlike Sam, and that he lived too far away from them. 'Your home is in the east, but ours is here in the west. We thought we'd made your position safe before we'd left, so it should have been easy for you to maintain it. However, it's turned out exactly as I expected when you spared Hrafnkel's life: I thought you'd live to regret this bitterly. We urged you to have Hrafnkel killed – that seemed the sensible thing to do – but you insisted on having it your own way. Now it's clear how much shrewder Hrafnkel is than you, for he left you in peace until he could first get rid of the man he knew to be wiser than you. We've no wish to have anything more to do with your bad luck and we are not so eager to clash with Hrafnkel again that we want to risk our position for the second time. But the main reason for our refusal is that you live so far away, and we think it is rather too much to travel all the way to the Eastfjords. We'd like to invite you and your family to come here and put yourselves under our care, for you'll find it less uncomfortable than living so close to Hrafnkel.'

Sam said he couldn't be bothered to move house from the Eastfjords, and the only help they could give was to do as he asked. Then he told them he wanted to make ready for the ride back home, and asked them to exchange horses with him, which they did willingly.

The brothers wanted to give Sam fine gifts but he wouldn't accept them, and said they were small-minded men. Then he set out for home, and they parted on bad terms. Sam settled down on his farm and lived there till old age, without ever, for the rest of his life, being able to avenge himself on Hrafnkel.

Hrafnkel remained on his farm and for some years he

enjoyed great prestige. He didn't live to a great age and died in his bed. His burial mound stands in Hrafnkelsdale, north of Adalbol. His sons inherited his authority and chieftaincy. They met to divide the property between them but agreed to own the chieftaincy jointly. Thorir got Hrafnkelsstead and lived there, but Asbjorn took charge of Adalbol, and people thought them both men of mettle.

And so ends the saga of Hrafnkel.

THORSTEIN THE STAFF-STRUCK

THERE was a man called Thorarin who lived at Sunnudale; he was old and nearly blind. He had been a fierce
viking in his younger years, and even in his old age he was
very hard to deal with. He had an only son, Thorstein, who
was a tall man, powerful but even-tempered; he worked so
hard on his father's farm that three other men could hardly
have done any better. Thorarin had little money, but a
good many weapons. He and his son owned some breeding
horses and that was their main source of income, for the
young colts they sold never failed in spirit or strength.

Bjarni of Hof[1] had a servant called Thord who looked
after his riding horses and was considered very good at the
job. Thord was an arrogant man and would never let anyone forget the fact that he was in the service of a chieftain.
But this didn't make him a better man and added nothing
to his popularity. Bjarni also had two brothers working
for him who were called Thorhall and Thorvald, both
great scandalmongers about any gossip they heard in the
district.

Thorstein and Thord arranged a horse-fight for their
young stallions.[2] During the fight, Thord's horse started

1. Bjarni of Hof was the local chieftain, and the wealthiest and
most powerful farmer in the district. He plays an important role in
Vopnfirdinga Saga and figures also in *The Story of Gunnar Thid-
randi's Killer*. The author of the present story evidently takes it for
granted that his readers must be familiar with *Vopnfirdinga Saga*,
which explains why Bjarni of Hof is not formally introduced here, as
is the normal saga practice.

2. Horse-fights used to be a favourite sport in Iceland. Two
stallions were pitted against one another, and behind each of them

giving way, and when Thord realized he was losing, he struck Thorstein's horse a hard blow on the jaw. Thorstein saw this and hit back with an even heavier blow at Thord's horse, forcing it to back away. This got the spectators shouting with excitement. Then Thord aimed a blow at Thorstein with his horse-goad, hitting him so hard on the eye-brow that the skin broke and the lid fell hanging down over the eye. Thorstein tore a piece off his shirt and bandaged his head. He said nothing about what had happened, apart from asking people to keep this from his father. That should have been the end of the incident, but Thorvald and Thorhall kept jeering at Thorstein and gave him the nickname Staff-Struck.

One morning that winter just before Christmas, when the women at Sunnudale were getting up for their work, Thorstein went out to feed the cattle. He soon came back and lay down on a bench. His father, old Thorarin, came into the room and asked who was lying there. Thorstein told him.

'Why are you up so early, son?' said Thorarin.

Thorstein answered, 'It seems to me there aren't many men about to share the work with me.'

'Have you got a head-ache, son?' said Thorarin.

'Not that I've noticed,' said Thorstein.

'What can you tell me about the horse-fight last summer, son?' said Thorarin. 'Weren't you beaten senseless like a dog?'

'It's no credit to me if you call it a deliberate blow, not an accident,' said Thorstein.

Thorarin said, 'I'd never have thought I could have a coward for a son.'

---

there was a man equipped with a goad to prod them on. At these horse fights tempers would often run high, see *Njal's Saga*, Penguin Classics, 1960, p. 143, and *Laxdæla Saga*, Penguin Classics, 1969, pp. 130–31. Trained fighting horses were sometimes exported to Norway.

'Father,' said Thorstein, 'Don't say anything now that you'll live to regret later.'

'I'm not going to say as much as I've a mind to,' said Thorarin.

Thorstein got to his feet, seized his weapons and set off. He came to the stable where Thord was grooming Bjarni's horses, and when he saw Thord he said, 'I'd like to know, friend Thord, whether it was accidental when you hit me in the horse-fight last summer, or deliberate. If it was deliberate, you'll be willing to pay me compensation.'

'If only you were double-tongued,' said Thord, 'then you could easily speak with two voices and call the blow accidental with one and deliberate with the other. That's all the compensation you're getting from me.'

'In that case don't expect me to make this claim a second time,' said Thorstein.

With that he rushed at Thord and dealt him his death-blow. Then he went up to the house at Hof where he saw a woman standing outside the door. 'Tell Bjarni that a bull has gored Thord, his horse-boy,' he said to her, 'and also that Thord will be waiting for him at the stable.'

'Go back home, man,' she said. 'I'll tell Bjarni in my own good time.'

Thorstein went back home, and the woman carried on with her work.

After Bjarni had got up that morning and was sitting at table, he asked where Thord could be, and was told he had gone to see to the horses.

'I'd have thought he'd be back by now, unless something has happened to him,' said Bjarni.

The woman Thorstein had spoken to broke in. 'It's true what we women are often told, we're not very clever. Thorstein the Staff-Struck came here this morning and he said Thord had been gored by a bull and couldn't look

74

after himself. I didn't want to wake you, and then I forgot
all about it.'

Bjarni left the table, went over to the stable and found
Thord lying there, dead. Bjarni had him buried, then
brought a court action against Thorstein and had him
sentenced to outlawry for manslaughter. But Thorstein
stayed on at Sunnudale and worked for his father, and
Bjarni did nothing more about it.

One day in the autumn when the men of Hof were busy
singeing sheep's heads[3], Bjarni lay down on top of the kit-
chen wall to listen to their talk. Now the brothers Thorhall
and Thorvald started gossiping; 'It never occurred to us
when we came to live here with Killer-Bjarni[4] that we'd be
singeing lambs' heads while his outlaw Thorstein is singeing the heads of wethers. It would have been better for
Bjarni to have been more lenient with his kinsmen at Bodvarsdale and not to let his outlaw at Sunnudale act just
like his own equal. But "A wounded coward lies low", and
it's not likely that he'll ever wipe away this stain on his
honour.'

One of the men said, 'Those words were better left un-
said, the trolls must have twisted your tongue. I think
Bjarni simply isn't prepared to take the only breadwinner
at Sunnudale away from Thorstein's blind father and
other dependants there. I'll be more than surprised if you
singe many more lambs' heads here, or tattle on much
longer about the fight at Bodvarsdale.'

3. In Iceland, as in some other sheep-raising countries, sheep's
heads were (and still are) considered a great delicacy. The heads are
singed over a fire to remove all traces of wool before they are cleaned
and cooked.

4. The name Killer-Bjarni is an allusion to the fact that Bjarni
fought and killed some of his own kinsmen in the battle of Bodvarsdale which is mentioned in the following sentence. This event is
described in *Vopnfirdinga Saga*, and it is alluded to in *Ale-Hood*,
p. 91 below.

Then they went inside to have their meal, and after that to bed. Bjarni gave no sign that he had heard anything of what had been said. But early next morning he roused Thorhall and Thorvald and told them to ride over to Sunnudale and bring him Thorstein's severed head before mid-morning. 'I think you're more likely than anyone else to wipe away that stain from my honour, since I haven't the courage to do it for myself,' he said.

The brothers realized they had said too much, but they set off and went over to Sunnudale. Thorstein was standing in the doorway, sharpening a short sword. He asked them where they were going, and they told him they were looking for some horses. Thorstein said they didn't have very far to go. 'The horses are down by the fence.'

'We're not sure we'll be able to find them unless you tell us more precisely,' they said.

Thorstein came outside, and as they were walking together across the meadow, Thorvald raised his axe and rushed at him. But Thorstein pushed him back so hard that he fell, then ran him through with the short sword. Thorhall tried to attack Thorstein and went the same way as his brother. Thorstein tied them to their saddles, fixed the reins to the horses' manes, and drove them off.

The horses went back to Hof. Some of the servants there were out of doors and went inside to tell Bjarni that Thorvald and Thorhall had come back and their journey hadn't been wasted. Bjarni went outside and saw what had happened. He said nothing and had the two men buried. Then everything was quiet till after Christmas.

One evening after Bjarni and his wife Rannveig had gone to bed, she said to him, 'What do you think everyone in the district is talking about these days?'

'I couldn't say,' said Bjarni. 'In my opinion most people talk a lot of rubbish.'

'This is what people are mainly talking about now,' she continued: 'They're wondering how far Thorstein the Staff-Struck can go before you bother to take revenge. He's killed three of your servants, and your supporters are beginning to doubt whether you can protect them, seeing that you've failed to avenge this. You often take action when you shouldn't and hold back when you should.'

'It's the same old story,' said Bjarni, 'no one seems willing to learn from another man's lesson. Thorstein has never killed anyone without a good reason – but still, I'll think about your suggestion.'

With that they dropped the subject and slept through the night. In the morning Rannveig woke up as Bjarni was taking down his sword and shield. She asked him where he was going.

'The time has come for me to settle that matter of honour between Thorstein of Sunnudale and myself,' he said.

'How many men are you taking with you?' she asked.

'I'm not taking a whole army to attack Thorstein,' he said. 'I'm going alone.'

'You mustn't do that,' she said, 'risking your life against the weapons of that killer.'

'You're a typical woman,' said Bjarni, 'arguing against the very thing you were urging just a few hours ago! There's a limit to my patience, I can only stand so much taunting from you and others. And once my mind's made up, there's no point in trying to hold me back.'

Bjarni went over to Sunnudale. He saw Thorstein standing in the doorway, and they exchanged some words.

'You'll fight me in single combat,' said Bjarni, 'on that hillock over there in the home-meadow.'

'I'm in no way good enough to fight you,' said Thorstein. 'I give you my promise to leave the country with the first ship that sails abroad. I know a generous man like you

77

will provide my father with labour to run the farm if I go away.'

'You can't talk yourself out of this now,' said Bjarni.

'You'll surely let me go and see my father first,' said Thorstein.

'Certainly,' said Bjarni.

Thorstein went inside and told his father that Bjarni had come and challenged him to a duel.

The old man said, 'Anybody who offends a more power- ful man in his own district can hardly expect to wear out many more new shirts. In my opinion your offences are so serious, I can't find any excuse for you. So you'd better take your weapons and defend yourself the best you can. In my younger days I'd never have given way before some- one like Bjarni, great fighting-man though he may be. I'd much rather lose you than have a coward for a son.'

Thorstein went outside and walked with Bjarni up the hillock. They started fighting with determination and des- troyed each other's shield. When they had been fighting for a long time, Bjarni said to Thorstein, 'I'm getting very thirsty now, I'm not so used to hard work as you are.'

'Go down to the stream then and drink,' said Thorstein.

Bjarni did so, and laid the sword down beside him. Thorstein picked it up, examined it and said, 'You can't have been using this sword at Bodvarsdale.'

Bjarni said nothing, and they went back to the hillock. After they'd been fighting for a time, it became obvious to Bjarni that Thorstein was a highly skilled fighter, and the outcome seemed less certain than he'd expected.

'Everything seems to go wrong for me today,' he said. 'Now my shoe-thong's loose.'

'Tie it up then,' said Thorstein.

When Bjarni bent down to tie it, Thorstein went into the house and brought back two shields and a sword. He joined Bjarni on the hillock and said, 'Here's a sword and

shield my father sends you. The sword shouldn't get so
easily blunted as the one you've been using. And I don't
want to stand here any longer with no shield to protect me
against your blows. I'd very much like us to stop this game
now, for I'm afraid your good luck will prove stronger
than my bad luck. Every man wants to save his life, and I
would too, if I could.'

'There's no point in your trying to talk yourself out of
this,' said Bjarni. 'The fight must go on.'

'I wouldn't like to be the first to strike,' said Thorstein.

Then Bjarni struck at Thorstein, destroying his shield,
and Thorstein hacked down Bjarni's shield in return.

'That was a blow,' said Bjarni.

Thorstein replied, 'Yours wasn't any lighter.'

Bjarni said, 'Your sword seems to be biting much better
now than it was earlier.'

'I want to save myself from the foulest of luck if I possibly can,' said Thorstein. 'It scares me to have to fight you,
so I want you yourself to settle the matter between us.'

It was Bjarni's turn to strike. Both men had lost their
shields. Bjarni said, 'It would be a great mistake in one
stroke both to throw away good fortune and do wrong. In
my opinion I'd be fully paid for my three servants if you
took their place and served me faithfully.'

Thorstein said, 'I've had plenty of opportunity today to
take advantage of you, if my bad luck had been stronger
than your good luck. I'll never deceive you.'

'Now I can see what a remarkable man you must be,'
said Bjarni. 'You'll allow me to go inside to see your father
and tell him about this in my own words?'

'You can go if you want as far as I'm concerned,' said
Thorstein, 'but be on your guard.'

Bjarni went up to the bed-closet where Old Thorarin
was lying. Thorarin asked who was there, and Bjarni told
him.

'What's your news, friend Bjarni?' said Thorarin.

'The killing of Thorstein, your son,' said Bjarni.

'Did he put up any defence at all?' asked Thorarin.

'I don't think there's ever been a better fighter than your son, Thorarin,' said Bjarni.

'It's no wonder your opponents at Bodvarsdale found you so hard to deal with,' said Thorarin, 'seeing that you've overcome my son.'

Bjarni said, 'I want to invite you to come over to Hof and take the seat of honour there for the rest of your life. I'll be just like a son to you.'

'I'm in the same position now as any other pauper,' said Thorarin. 'Only a fool accepts a promise gladly, and promises of chieftains like yourself aren't usually honoured for more than a month after the event, while you're trying to console us. After that we're treated as ordinary paupers, though our grief doesn't grow any the less for that. Still, anyone who shakes hands on a bargain with a man of your character should be satisfied, in spite of other men's lessons. So I'd like to shake hands with you, and you'd better come into the bed-closet to me. Come closer now, for I'm an old man and trembling on my feet because of ill-health and old age. And I must admit, the loss of my son has upset me a bit.'

Bjarni went into the bed-closet and shook Thorarin by the hand. Then he realized the old man was groping for a short sword with the idea of thrusting it at him. Bjarni pulled back his hand and said, 'You merciless old rascal! I can promise you now you'll get what you deserve. Your son Thorstein is alive and well, and he'll come with me over to Hof, but you'll be given slaves to run the farm for you, and never suffer any want for the rest of your life.'

Thorstein went with Bjarni over to Hof, and stayed in his service for the rest of his life. He was considered a man of great courage and integrity. Bjarni kept his standing

and became better-liked and more self-controlled the older
he grew. He was a very trustworthy man. In the last years
of his life he became a devout Christian and went to Rome
on pilgrimage. He died on that journey, and is buried at a
town called Sutri,[5] just north of Rome.[6]

5. *Sutri*. The MSS have Vateri which is probably a scribal error.
The town Sutri is mentioned elsewhere in early Icelandic records.

6. The story concludes with the following genealogy (dates have
been added in brackets):

Bjarni had a fine progeny. He was the father of Beard-Broddi,
who figures in a number of sagas, and was the outstanding man of
his time.

Bjarni had a daughter called Halla, the mother of Gudrid, who
married Kolbein the Lawspeaker.

Bjarni had another daughter called Yngvild who married Thorstein Hallsson of Sida, and their son was Magnus, the father of Einar,
the father of Bishop Magnus (d. 1148). Thorstein and Yngvild had
another son called Amundi, who married Sigrid the daughter of
Thorgrim the Blind. Amundi had a daughter called Hallfrid, the
mother of Amundi, the father of Gudmund the father of the chieftain Magnus, of Thora the wife of Thorvald Gizurarson (d. 1237),
and of the other Thora the mother of Orm of Svinafell (d. 1239).

Amundi had another daughter called Gudrun, the mother of
Thordis, the mother of Helga, the mother of Gudny Bodvar's daughter, the mother of the Sturlusons: Thord (d. 1235), Sighvat (d. 1237),
and Snorri (d. 1241).

Amundi had a third daughter called Rannveig, the mother of
Stein, the father of Gudrun, the mother of Arnfrid who was married
to Stout-Helgi.

Amundi had a fourth daughter who was called Thorkatla, the
mother of Arnbjorg, the mother of the Priest Finn, of Thorgeir, and
of Thurid.

There were a good many outstanding people descended from them.
And so ends the *Story of Thorstein the Staff-Struck*.

ALE-HOOD

1. THE FIRE

THERE was a man called Thorhall who lived at Thorhallsstead in Blawoods.[1] He was a wealthy man and getting
on in years when this story happened. Thorhall was small
and ugly, with no particular skills except for being a good
carpenter and blacksmith. He used to make money at the
Althing brewing ale, and through this he got to know all
the important people, who bought more ale than most. As
often happens, not everybody thought much of the ale, and
the man who sold it wasn't always well liked either. Thorhall wasn't open-handed – indeed he was said to be rather
stingy. His eye-sight was poor, and he used to wear a hood,
particularly at the Althing; and since the people there
couldn't always remember his name, they started calling
him Ale-Hood, and the nickname stuck.

One autumn Ale-Hood went to a certain wood of his, intending to make charcoal. This wood lay to the north of
Hrafnabjorg and east of Langahlid. He spent several days
there getting the logs ready, then he started burning the
charcoal. During the night he kept watch over the charcoal
pits, but just before morning he dozed off and the fire in
the pits flared up and caught the nearest branches. Soon
they were all ablaze, and the fire reached the wood and
started raging through it. Then a gale blew up.

Ale-Hood woke up and thought he was lucky to be alive.
The fire kept raging through the trees, destroying first Ale-
Hood's own woodland then the copses among the lava

1. Thorhallsstead in Blawoods was situated close to Thingvellir
where the Althing was held annually, late in June.

fields when it reached the adjacent woods, the part now known as Svidning.[2]

One wood destroyed was called Goda Wood. It belonged to six chieftains, first Snorri the Priest, then Gudmund Eyjolfsson, Skapti the Lawspeaker, Thorkel Geitisson, Eyjolf (the son of Thord Gellir), and finally Thorkel Fringe (the son of Ore-Bjorn)[3]. They'd bought this woodland for their own use at the Althing.

After the fire Ale-Hood went back home, and the news began to spread from place to place. Skapti was the first of the wood-owners to hear of the loss, and in the autumn he sent word with some travellers north to Eyjafjord telling Gudmund about the fire and pointing out to him too that this could be a profitable law-suit. Similar messages were sent to the chieftains in the west who owned shares in the wood. During the winter all the owners exchanged messages, and the six chieftains agreed to meet at the Althing and take joint action. Skapti was to start the proceedings as he lived nearest.

In the spring, at summons days, Skapti rode off with a number of men and served a summons on Ale-Hood for burning the wood, on pain of full outlawry.[4] Ale-Hood blustered and threatened, and said Skapti wouldn't be so boastful at the Althing when Ale-Hood's friends were around. Skapti said nothing and rode away.

2. Literally 'The scorched place'.

3. All these six chieftains are well known from other sources, and were among the most powerful men in Iceland during the first decades of the 11th century. They all held the rank of chieftain (*goði*: hence the place name *Goðaskógr*, Goda Wood).

4. An Althing summons had to be served on certain days, four weeks before the assembly convened. See e.g. *Njal's Saga*, Penguin Classics, 1960, p. 127n. – According to early Icelandic law the penalty for burning someone's woodland accidentally was either a fine or 'the lesser outlawry', i.e. a three years' banishment. But wilful destruction of woodland was a very serious crime and carried with it the maximum sentence of 'full outlawry', i.e. for life.

In the summer the six chieftains who owned the wood went to the Althing where they all met and decided to prosecute. They agreed that unless they were given self-judgement,[5] they'd ask for heavy damages.

Ale-Hood came to the Althing too, hoping to sell his ale. He went to see the friends who used to buy ale from him and asked them for help. He offered to sell them ale but everyone gave the same answer – that Ale-Hood had never shown them any favours in their dealings with him, and they were not getting involved in his law-suit against such powerful opposition. No one was willing to help him or even to buy his ale and it looked to him as if the situation was becoming tricky. He went from booth to booth and always got the same answer to his appeal for help till he didn't have much of his pride and arrogance left.

2. THE BENEFACTOR

One day Ale-Hood went to ask for help at the booth of Thorstein Hallsson[6] and Thorstein gave him the same answer as everybody else.

Thorstein had a brother-in-law called Broddi Bjarnason, who was sitting next to him – Broddi was in his early twenties when this happened. When Thorstein refused to help him, Ale-Hood went out of the booth.

Broddi said, 'It seems to me, brother-in-law, that this man hasn't the look of a criminal. It's very mean-minded of these people who think themselves so important, to want to make an outlaw of him. You'll agree with me it would be a fine gesture to help him.'

Thorstein said, 'You can help him then, since you're so

5. *Sjálf-dœmi*. A plaintiff claiming damages was sometimes given the right to decide on the amount to be paid to him.

6. He figures in *The Saga of Thorstein Hallsson* and *The Dream of Thorstein Hallsson*.

keen, but I promise to give you as much backing this time as I always do.'

Broddi asked someone to go outside and fetch Ale-Hood. The man did as he was told, and when he came out he saw Ale-Hood leaning against the wall of the booth, crying his eyes out. The man told him to come back into the booth and stop moaning. 'You'd better not be snivelling when you meet Thorstein,' he said.

Ale-Hood now started weeping for joy, and went inside. When they came before Thorstein, Broddi spoke up. 'I think Thorstein is willing to help you, for in his opinion this is a trumped-up case. You couldn't possibly have saved the other woods, once your own had been burnt down.'

Ale-Hood said, 'Who's this good man talking to me?'

'My name's Broddi,' he said.

'Is this Broddi Bjarnason?' said Ale-Hood.

'It is,' said Broddi.

'When I look at you I can see you're a real gentleman, not like most people, and it's just what I'd expect from your family,' said Ale-Hood.

Ale-Hood continued in this vein for some time, his words becoming braver and braver the longer he spoke.

'Well, Broddi, your turn's come to give him some real help,' said Thorstein. 'You're very keen to do so, and he keeps showering you with compliments.'

Broddi got to his feet, and went out of the booth along with a good many men. He took Ale-Hood aside for a private talk, then they went over to the assembly plain where a crowd of people had been attending the Court of Legislature. Soon everyone left, except Gudmund and Skapti who stayed behind to discuss a few legal points. Broddi and his companions walked about the plain, but Ale-Hood went over to the Court of Legislature, and threw himself at the feet of Skapti and Gudmund. 'What a

stroke of luck to have found you, glorious masters,' he said.
'Help me now, good people, though I don't deserve it, for
without your help I haven't a chance.'

It would take too long to repeat everything that Ale-
Hood said, for he kept on talking and grovelling.

Gudmund said to Skapti, 'What a miserable exhibition
the man's making of himself.'

Skapti said, 'What's become of your pride, Ale-Hood?
You didn't expect you'd have to come to me with your
troubles when we served you the summons in the spring.
Have you found the chieftains helpful, the ones you
threatened me with in the spring?'

'I was out of my mind then,' said Ale-Hood, 'even worse
than mad, not wanting you to give your own judgement in
the case. Don't mention the chieftains to me, they lose
their nerve as soon as they set eyes on you. How happy
I'd be if only I could leave it to you to settle the issue! But
is there any chance of that now? You've certainly a good
excuse, friend Skapti, not to want it, for you must be very
angry with me. What an utter fool I was not to take your
offer to judge the case! Now I daren't face these terrible
men, they'll kill me on sight unless you two come to my
rescue.'

He kept repeating the same thing and telling them how
happy he would be if they were to adjudicate the case. 'I
think my money would be in the best of hands if you were
to have it,' he said.

Gudmund spoke to Skapti. 'I don't think this man de-
serves to be outlawed. Wouldn't it be better to grant him
his wish and choose arbitrators to settle the matter? But
I'm not so sure how the other plaintiffs will take it.'

'Well, my dear fellows,' said Ale-Hood. 'I'm sure you'll
grant me your protection when this is all over.'

Skapti said, 'The conduct of this law-suit is my business
as I'm in charge of the prosecution. Gudmund and I will

risk arbitrating the case, Ale-Hood, to get it over and done
with. I think this is how we can best help you out of your .
difficulties.'

Ale-Hood got to his feet and shook them by the hand.
He named witnesses, one after another, and as soon as
people realized that witnesses were being named they
started crowding up. The first witnesses Ale-Hood named
were Broddi and his companions.

Skapti said, 'The defendant in this law-suit has invited
Gudmund and myself to arbitrate, and although all those
who suffered the loss had agreed only to accept self-judgement, Gudmund and I are willing to grant Ale-Hood this
much that we two rather than any other men shall arbitrate in the matter, if he agrees. You are to stand as witnesses that damages only shall be awarded, and there'll be no
outlawry. I solemnly declare that I drop the charge on
which I summonsed him in the spring.'

Then they dissolved the handshake.

Skapti said to Gudmund. 'Why shouldn't we get this
over and done with now?'

'That's a good idea,' said Gudmund.

Ale-Hood said, 'You mustn't be so hasty, for I've not
decided to choose you rather than someone else.'

Gudmund said, 'It was stipulated that Skapti and I
should arbitrate unless you specified some others from
among the plaintiffs.'

Ale-Hood said, 'I've never agreed these men should
arbitrate, it was stipulated at the handshake that I could
choose any two men I wanted.'

The matter was referred to the men who'd been acting
as witnesses to the agreement. The followers of Gudmund
and Skapti disagreed violently as to what had been stipulated, but Broddi and his men gave a clear decision that
the stipulation had been just as Ale-Hood had said; he
was to choose the arbitrators.

Then Skapti said, 'Where did you think this up, Ale-Hood? You're holding your head higher now than a few moments ago. Whom do you want to appoint as arbitrators?'

Ale-Hood said, 'I don't need much time to think it over. I choose Thorstein Hallsson and his brother-in-law Broddi Bjarnason. I think the case will then be in better hands than if you and Gudmund were to arbitrate.'

Skapti agreed the matter would then be in very capable hands if these men were to arbitrate. 'Our claim is both urgent and just, and they are such shrewd men they'll fully realize how harshly you must be dealt with.'

Ale-Hood joined Broddi's following, and everyone went back to the booths.

3. THE INSULTS

The verdict was to be announced the following day, and Thorstein and Broddi started considering the case. Thorstein wanted to award higher damages than Broddi, so Broddi said it would be best if Thorstein made the award he wanted and then announced his findings himself. Broddi asked him which he would prefer: to announce the verdict or provide the answers, should someone object to their findings. Thorstein said he'd rather announce the verdict than exchange abuse with the chieftains. He said too that Ale-Hood wouldn't have long to wait for the decision, and that he'd have to pay the entire fine then and there at the Law Rock. Then they went over to the Law Rock, and when other legal matters had been dealt with, Thorstein asked whether the chieftains who had brought the charges against Ale-Hood were present. 'I've been told that Broddi and I are to assess the damages. We're going to announce our verdict now if you're ready to hear it,' said Thorstein.

The chieftains said they were confident the verdict would be a just one.

Then Thorstein said, 'In our opinion your woodland was of no great value, the woods themselves were worth very little and too remote to be of any real use to you. It was sheer avarice for wealthy men like you to add to your property in this way. It was not within Ale-Hood's power to save your wood, once he had destroyed his own. This was an accident, but since it has been referred to arbitration some damages must be awarded. Six of you owned this wood, and we are awarding six ells of homespun cloth' to each of you, the whole amount to be paid up here and now.'

Broddi had already cut up the cloth so he was ready for this. He threw a piece to each of them and said, 'I call this a tribute to the craven.'

Skapti said, 'It's quite obvious, Broddi, that you are trying hard to provoke us. You've gone out of your way to get involved in this dispute, and you're far from reluctant to make enemies of us. Other law-suits will prove easier for us I shouldn't wonder.'

Broddi said, 'You'll have to win a great deal of money from other law-suits, Skapti, before you make up for the damages your kinsman Orm got out of you after you'd composed a love-song about his wife. That wasn't a very virtuous thing to do, and you were made to pay for it dearly.'[8]

Thorkel Fringe said, 'That's a stupid mistake for a man like Broddi. Just to have Ale-Hood's friendship, or his bribes, he's prepared to turn opponents into enemies.'

Broddi said, 'It's no mistake to want to keep one's integ-

7. The total amount Ale-Hood is asked to pay the six chieftains comes to less than half the price of a cow.

8. According to early Icelandic law it was a serious offence to address a love-poem to a woman, even to an unmarried one.

rity, and it makes no difference whether you're the better man, or Ale-Hood. But you yourself made a big mistake last spring when you rode to the local assembly. You didn't notice the fat stallion that Steingrim had till it was up your backside. That skinny mare you were on faltered under you, didn't she, and I've never been able to make up my mind whether it was you or the mare that got it. Everybody could see how long you were stuck there, the stallion's legs had got such a grip on your cloak.'

Eyjolf Thordarson said, 'It's true enough, this man has cheated us out of our catch, and on top of that he's piling his filthy abuse on us.'

Broddi said, 'I've never cheated you, you were cheated when you went north to Skagafjord to steal the oxen from Thorkel Eiriksson, and Starri of Goddale chased after you. When you reached Vatnsdale and saw who was after you, you were so scared you turned yourself into a mare, a pretty outrageous thing to do. Starri and his men drove back the cattle so it can't be denied, he cheated you.'[9]

Then Snorri the Priest said, 'Anything would be better for us than to exchange abuse with Broddi, but let's make sure we remember what kind of friendship Broddi has shown us, and never forget it.'

Broddi said, 'You can't have much sense of priorities if you will insist on taking revenge on me rather than avenging your father.'[10]

Thorkel Geitisson said, 'It strikes me that all you've in-

9. This is one of the rare instances in the Icelandic sagas where a cattle-raid is mentioned, but cattle-raids are a common theme in the early Irish sagas. See *Laxdæla Saga*, Penguin Classics, 1969. pp. 37 and 83–4.

10. In *Njal's Saga*, Penguin Classics, 1960. p. 246, Skarphedin makes a similar insinuation. Snorri was born shortly after his father, Thorgrim, had been murdered by Gisli Sursson who was Thorgrim's brother-in-law and Snorri's uncle. This tragic event is described in *Gisli's Saga* (Ch. 16). See also *Eyrbyggja Saga* (Ch. 12).

herited from the man whose name you were given is to make all the trouble you can for everyone. Nobody's going to put up with this sort of thing for long, and maybe you'll have to pay for it with your life.'

Broddi said, 'We can't gain anything, kinsman, by shouting in public about our people's bad luck. There's no point in denying what everyone knows, that Brodd-Helgi was killed, but I've been told your own father paid the same high price. I think if you had any sense of touch in your fingers you'd find the scars my father marked you with at Bodvarsdale.'[11]

With that they parted, and went back to their booths. Ale-Hood is now out of the story.

4. RECONCILIATION

Next day Broddi walked over to Thorkel Geitisson's booth, went in and spoke to Thorkel, who was in a bad mood and made no reply.

Broddi said, 'The reason I've come to see you, kinsman, is that I realize how ill-chosen my words to you were. Please, blame that on the silliness of my age, and don't let our kinship suffer because of it. Here's an ornamented sword I want to give you, and I'd like you to accept an invitation to come and visit me in the summer. I promise you I've no treasures in my hands finer than the ones I'm proposing to give you.'

Thorkel accepted this gladly and said he would very much like them to observe their kinship properly. Then Broddi went back to his booth.

The day before the Althing broke up Broddi happened to go west across the river, and at the bridge he met Gudmund Eyjolfsson. Neither greeted the other, but as they

11. See p. 75 above.

were drawing apart, Gudmund turned back and said, 'What route are you taking back home from the Althing?'

Broddi turned round and said, 'If you want to know, I'll be riding north over to Kjol to Skagafjord, from there to Eyjafjord, then through Ljosawater Pass, and so to Mywater and across Modrudale Moor.'

Gudmund said, 'Keep your promise then and ride through Ljosawater Pass.'

Broddi said, 'I'll keep my promise all right. Could it be you mean to stop me getting through the Pass? You've made a bad miscalculation if you try to stop me and my companions from riding through Ljosawater Pass, seeing the honour you lost when you didn't bother to defend the narrow pass in your backside.'

With that they parted, but their words were soon known to everyone at the Althing. When Thorkel Geitisson heard about this he went to see Broddi and asked him to ride either the Sand route or the eastern route.[12]

Broddi said, 'I'll ride the way I told Gudmund, he'll call me a coward if I take a different route.'

Thorkel said, 'In that case I'll go with you, kinsman, and my small band of men.'

Broddi said he'd like that very much for he considered it an honour to have Thorkel's company. When they were going north across Oxnadale Moor, Thorkel's father-in-law Einar Eyjolfsson joined them, so they rode with him to Thverriver and spent a night there. Einar accompanied them on their way with a large following, and didn't turn back till they got to Skjalfandi River. He went back home and Thorkel and Broddi kept going till they reached their farms east in Vopnafjord.

In the summer Thorkel went to see his kinsman Broddi

12. The Sand route is the one taken by Sam to Althing, and the eastern route the one that Hrafnkel followed. See *Hrafnkel's Saga*, Ch. 8.

and accepted some excellent gifts from him. For the rest of their lives they respected their kinship and stayed good friends.

And so we end the story of Ale-Hood.

HREIDAR THE FOOL

THERE was a man called Thord,[1] a small, good-looking man. He had a brother, Hreidar, who was ugly and so stupid he could scarcely take care of himself. Hreidar was an exceptionally fast runner, very strong and even-tempered. He stayed at home, but Thord was a sea-going trader and a retainer of King Magnus who thought very highly of him.[2]

One day when Thord was getting his ship ready at Eyjafjord, his brother Hreidar came to see him. Thord saw him and asked why he'd come.

'I wouldn't be here if I hadn't some business with you,' said Hreidar.

'What do you want then,' asked Thord.

'I want to go abroad,' said Hreidar.

'I don't think you're quite the man for travelling abroad,' said Thord. 'Rather than let you go, I'll gladly give you all my share in our inheritance, that's twice as much as I've invested in my trading.'

'I'd be very stupid,' said Hreidar, 'if I took that money just to be left in the lurch and lose your guidance. I can't manage anything on my own, and all sorts of people would be cheating me out of our money. And it wouldn't

1. *The son of Thorgrim, the son of Hreidar whom Killer-Glum killed.* Killer-Glum is the eponymous hero of *Killer-Glum's Saga*.

2. King Magnus the Good (d. 1047) was the son of Saint Olaf (d. 1030); his life is described in *The Saga of Magnus the Good*. The following incidents are evidently supposed to have taken place during the year 1046–47 when Norway was ruled jointly by King Magnus and his uncle King Harald Hardradi (d. 1066). See *King Harald's Saga* and *Halldor Snorrason* below.

be much fun for you to get involved, once I'd had a go at
the ones who were after my money. As for myself, I'd probably finish up battered and crippled. The truth is, you'll
find it pretty hard to hold me back once I've made up my
mind to go.'

'You could be right,' said Thord, 'but don't tell anyone
you're going.'

Hreidar gave his promise, but they'd hardly parted
when he began telling anyone willing to listen that he was
going abroad with his brother. Everyone criticized Thord
for taking such an idiot abroad.

When they were ready to sail they put out to sea and
had a good passage. They landed at Bergen, and Thord
wasted no time in asking whether the king was in residence. He was told King Magnus was in town; the king, in
fact, had just arrived and didn't want to be disturbed that
day as he needed a rest after his journey.

People soon noticed Hreidar, who stood out from everyone else: a tall, ugly man, and glad to chat with anyone he
saw.

Early the following morning, before the rest of the crew
were awake, Hreidar got up and shouted: 'Wake up,
brother! A sleeping man's an ignorant man too! I've news
for you, I've just heard a peculiar noise.'

'What was it like?' asked Thord.

'It sounded like some beast,' said Hreidar. 'It was a loud
shrill noise, but I've no idea what it could have been.'

'Don't be a fool,' said Thord. 'It must have been a trumpet.'

'What's the meaning of it?' said Hreidar.

Thord said, 'It's the usual thing to sound the trumpets
for a meeting, or the launching of a ship.'

'What are these meetings held for?' asked Hreidar.

'To settle serious disputes,' said Thord, 'and to make
any announcement the king sees fit to make to the people.'

'Will the king be there at this meeting?' asked Hreidar.

'I should think so,' said Thord.

'Then I'd better be there too,' said Hreidar. 'First thing, I'd like to go where I could see a really big crowd of people.'

'I couldn't agree with you less,' said Thord. 'I'd much rather you stayed away from large crowds, and I'm certainly not going myself.'

'It's no good talking like that,' said Hreidar. 'The two of us must go. You wouldn't want me to go there all by myself, and you can't stop me.'

Off ran Hreidar, and Thord realized he would have to go too, so he went after him, but Hreidar ran so fast that soon there was a long distance between them. When he saw how slowly Thord was going, Hreidar stopped and said, 'What I say is, it's a bad handicap to be small, because small men are never strong. Still, even a small man could be a good runner, but that you're obviously not. Better if you'd been less handsome and as quick on your feet as other men.'

Thord said, 'I doubt if my weakness suits me any the worse than your strength does you.'

'Let's grip each other's hands,' said Hreidar.

They did so, and after they'd walked for a while, Thord's hand became so numb he had to let go; he felt this wasn't a friendly contest because Hreidar was too rough. Hreidar set off again and ran till he came to a certain hillock. He stopped there and stared in all directions till he sighted a large crowd at the meeting. When Thord caught up with him, he said, 'Let's go together, brother.' Hreidar agreed, and when they came to the meeting a good many people who knew Thord were there to welcome him. King Magnus was told Thord had arrived. Thord presented himself before the king and greeted him courteously. The king returned the greeting in a friendly way.

The brothers had got separated after they came to the meeting, and people started poking fun at Hreidar and pushing him about. He talked a great deal and laughed out loud which made everyone even more amused and more eager to tease him; the crowd kept blocking his way.

The king asked Thord the news, and then he inquired what passengers had travelled with him and whether he wanted them to come and stay at court with him.

'My brother joined me on this trip,' said Thord.

'He must be a fine man,' said the king, 'if he's anything like you.'

'He's not like me,' said Thord.

The king said, 'Still, he may be a good man. In what particular way is he unlike you?'

Thord said, 'He's a big-built man, ugly and with the look of a criminal, and immensely strong; but he's very even-tempered.'

'He may still be a good man in other ways,' said the king.

'As a child people didn't think him very bright,' said Thord.

'I'm more interested to know what he's like now,' said the king. 'Can he look after himself?'

'Hardly,' said Thord.

'Why did you take him abroad then?' asked the king.

Thord said, 'My lord, Hreidar and I share everything equally between us, but he can't take care of his money and doesn't take the slightest interest in it. The only favour he has ever asked me was to come abroad with me, and I didn't think it fair to refuse him just this one thing, since he lets me have my way in everything else. Anyway, I thought it would bring him good luck if he met you.'

'I'd like to meet him,' said the king.

'All right,' said Thord. 'But just now he seems to have been knocked about a bit.'

The king sent someone for Hreidar, and when he was

97

told the king wanted to see him, he began to stride around
in a very arrogant manner, knocking against everything
that came in his way, for he wasn't used to being summoned to a royal presence. Hreidar was wearing breeches
down to the ankles, and had a grey cloak thrown over his
shoulders. He came before the king, knelt down to him
and greeted him courteously.

The king laughed and said, 'If you've any business with
me, let me know right away. After you, there are others
who want to see me urgently.'

Hreidar said, 'I think my business is more urgent than
theirs. I wanted to get a look at you, Sir.'

'Are you satisfied then,' said the king, 'now that you
have looked at me?'

'Well, yes,' said Hreidar. 'But I don't think I've seen
enough of you.'

'What can we do about that?' said the king. 'Do you
want me to stand up?'

'I would like you to do that,' said Hreidar.

The king got upon his feet and said, 'Now you can see
me close enough.'

'Not quite close enough,' said Hreidar, 'though it's a lot
better than before.'

'Would you like me to take off my cloak?' asked the
king.

'Yes, I'd like that,' said Hreidar.

'Before I do that I think we should talk this over,' said
the king. 'You Icelanders are sometimes very smart, and
for all I know you may be trying to make fun of me, and I
can't have that.'

Hreidar said, 'No one could possibly make fun of you,
my lord, or try to trick you in any way.'

The king took off his cloak, and said, 'Now you can look
at me as closely as you want.'

'I'll do that,' said Hreidar.

He walked round the king, muttering over and over again, 'Splendid, splendid.'

The king asked, 'Have you seen enough of me?'

Hreidar said, 'Yes, I have.'

'What do you think of me then?' said the king.

'My brother Thord wasn't exaggerating when he described your good points,' said Hreidar.

'Can you find any fault with me which other people haven't noticed before?' said the king.

'I don't want to find any fault with you,' said Hreidar, 'and in fact I can't find one now. For anyone who had the choice would want to be exactly like yourself.'

'You're overdoing it,' said the king.

'Other people must be taking pretty great risks, praising you,' said Hreidar, 'if it isn't true what I think of you and what I was telling you just now.'

The king said, 'Try to find a fault, just a small one.'

'The only one I can think of,' said Hreidar, 'is that one of your eyes lies a bit higher than the other.'

'There's only one man ever pointed that out before,' said the king, 'and that was my uncle Harald.[3] Now give me a fair chance and let me have a go at you. Take off your coat so that I can have a look.'

Hreidar took off his cloak. He had large ugly hands, terribly dirty, since he hadn't bothered to wash them properly. The king took a close look at him.

Then Hreidar said, 'Sir, what fault can you find with me?'

'I don't think there was ever a man born uglier than you,' said the king.

'That's just what people keep saying,' said Hreidar. 'But do I have any good points in me as far as you can judge?'

'Well,' said the king, 'your brother Thord tells me that you are even-tempered.'

3. King Harald Hardradi was the half-brother of St Olaf, King Magnus's father.

'That's true,' said Hreidar, 'but I don't feel happy about it.'

'One day you'll lose your temper,' said the king.

'Thank you for saying that,' said Hreidar. 'How long shall I have to wait till then?'

'I couldn't tell you exactly,' said the king, 'but probably some time this winter if my guess is right.'

'Thank you, my lord,' said Hreidar.

The king said, 'What are you good at?'

Hreidar said, 'I've never tried to find out, so I don't know.'

'I think you could be clever with your hands,' said the king.

'Well, thanks,' said Hreidar. 'It must be true if you say so. What I need now is a place to stay for the winter.'

The king said, 'You're welcome to stay here at court, but I think it would be better for you to keep away from the crowd.'

Hreidar said, 'Maybe. But even where there aren't many people about, something is bound to be repeated, particularly if it's a joke. I'm not discreet, I talk a lot, so maybe people will repeat my words to others, making fun of me and exaggerating out of all proportion what I'd been joking about. Safer for me to be staying where someone like my brother Thord could keep an eye on me, even if there are a lot of people about, than to stay where there's no one to put things right.'

The king said, 'You'd better do as you like then. You and your brother can both come and stay at court, if that's what you want.'

The moment the king had spoken, Hreidar ran off to tell anyone who bothered to listen to him how well he had got on with the king. Then he told his brother Thord that the king was allowing him to stay at court.

'In that case you'd better fit yourself out properly,' said

Thord. 'Get the best in weapons and clothes. That's not only the right thing to do, we can afford it. Most people seem to improve a lot when they put on fine clothes, and it is even more important to dress well in a royal house than anywhere else. And then the retainers would be less likely to make fun of you.'

'You're badly mistaken if you think I'll start wearing fancy clothes,' said Hreidar.

'Then the homespun will have to do,' said Thord.

'That would be better,' said Hreidar.

When Thord's suggestion had been carried out and Hreidar had put on proper clothing of homespun cloth and cleaned himself thoroughly, he looked a different man. He was still ugly, with a wry face, but now there was something valiant about him. All the same, he was marked out from everyone else and as soon as he came to court with his brother, the retainers started poking fun at him. They teased and bantered him in every conceivable way, and soon they discovered how ready he was to talk. His conversation was full of surprises, and he gave the retainers a lot of entertainment. Hreidar laughed at anything they said, but he always got the better of them in the end for he had a lively sense of humour. When they realized that he was an exceptionally strong man and not inclined to give way, whatever they did to him, they gradually stopped mocking him. Hreidar stayed at court for a while.

At this time there were two rulers in Norway, King Magnus and King Harald. Trouble had broken out between them, as one of King Magnus's retainers had killed one of King Harald's men. A peace meeting had been arranged between the kings to try to settle the issue.

When Hreidar heard that King Magnus was going to meet King Harald, he went to see him and said, 'I'd like to ask you a favour.'

'What do you want?'

'I'd like to go to the peace meeting,' said Hreidar. 'I'm not a widely travelled man, and I'm curious to see two kings together at the same place.'

'What you're saying is true,' said the king. 'You're not a widely travelled man. All the same, I've no intention of letting you go, for it would be a great risk for you to be exposed to King Harald's men. If the meeting were to cause you or anyone else any trouble, I'm afraid you might get into a rage. I know you want to go but I'd rather you didn't.'

'Very intriguing,' said Hreidar. 'I'm certainly going if I can expect to lose my temper there.'

'Would you go even without my leave?' said the king.

'Yes, I would.'

'Do you really think you can treat me just as you treat your brother Thord? You always get your own way with him.'

'I'll get on even better with you,' said Hreidar, 'you are so much shrewder than he is.'

The king realized that Hreidar would go even without his leave and if so in someone else's company. He was very much against this for he didn't know what might happen to Hreidar if he were on his own. So he allowed Hreidar to come along with him. Hreidar was given a horse and as soon as they set off Hreidar started riding so hard that his horse faltered. When the king heard about this, he said, 'That was a bit of luck. Someone must take Hreidar back home, he can't go any farther.'

'I'm not going to be stopped by a horse giving out,' said Hreidar. 'I wouldn't be a very good runner if I couldn't keep pace with you.'

They continued their journey, and some of the retainers tried to race their horses against Hreidar as they thought it would be fun to test how fast he could run, when he'd boasted so much of his speed. But he outran every horse that was raced against him, and he repeated that he didn't deserve to go to the meeting if he couldn't keep pace with them. As a result some of the men were forced to stay behind, since their horses were worn out.

When they arrived at the meeting place, King Magnus said to Hreidar, 'Stay close by me. Sit right next to me and don't go away. I'm afraid something may happen when King Harald's men see you.'

Hreidar said he'd do as the king asked. 'The closer I am to you, the better I like it,' he said.

Soon afterwards the kings met in private to discuss their business. When King Harald's men saw Hreidar strutting about, they thought this looked very promising for they'd heard some stories about him. While the kings were in conclave, Hreidar went to join King Harald's men, and they took him to a certain wood near by. There they started teasing him and knocking him about a bit. Sometimes he would fly away from them light as a bundle of straw, and sometimes he stood as firm as a rock and bounced them back. As the play went on, they grew rougher and rougher, and started throwing axe handles at him and scabbards. The nail-studded point of a scabbard caught him in the face, grazing it. He was still pretending to enjoy the game and kept on laughing, so they started playing even rougher than before.

Then Hreidar said, 'Now we've had a good deal of fun for a while, and the time has come to stop, for I'm getting tired of this. So let's go back to your king. I want to meet him.'

'We'll not have that,' they said. 'A devil like you mustn't be allowed to set eyes on our king. We're going to kill you right now.'

He didn't like the sound of this for he saw they were serious, and at this point he got really angry. He seized the man who had been the roughest with him, lifted him, and then banged him down head first, knocking his brains out and killing him instantly. The others thought that Hreidar must be superhuman in strength and cleared out. They ran over to King Harald and told him that one of his men had been killed.

'You must kill the man who did this,' said the king.

'That's not so easy,' they said, 'he got away.'

Meanwhile, Hreidar went back to King Magnus.

'Do you know what it's like to lose your temper?' said the king.

'Yes,' he said, 'now I know.'

'How did you like it?' said the king. 'I remember how anxious you were to find out.'

'I didn't like it at all,' said Hreidar. 'What I really wanted was to kill every one of them.'

'I often felt you'd get really angry,' said the king. 'I've decided to send you to one of my chieftains, Eyvind, of the Uplands, and he'll protect you against King Harald. I don't think it would be safe for you to stay any longer here at court; my uncle Harald is a very cunning man, and it would be hard to guard you against him. Come back to me when I send for you.'

Hreidar set off and travelled all the way to the Uplands, and Eyvind took him in as the king had asked.

The kings reached an agreement about the original issue, and there was a full settlement. But they couldn't see eye to eye on Hreidar's case. Magnus argued that the men who had provoked Hreidar were responsible and that they'd forfeited their impunity, so the slain man had been at fault and no compensation should be paid for him. King Harald, on the other hand, demanded compensation for his retainer, and the kings parted without a settlement.

A little later King Harald was told where Hreidar was staying. He set out with sixty men and arrived at Eyvind's farm early one morning, hoping to take him by surprise.

But he didn't succeed, for Eyvind was ready and waiting for him. He'd gathered forces in secret, and kept them hiding in the woods near the farm. Eyvind was to warn them with a certain sign as soon as Harald arrived and their help was needed.

Just before Harald came, Hreidar asked Eyvind to give him some silver and gold.

'Are you a skilled craftsman, then?' asked Eyvind.

'King Magnus said I was,' replied Hreidar. 'Apart from that I have no proof, for I've never put it to the test. But he wouldn't have said it unless he knew for certain, so I believe him.'

'What a strange fellow you are!' said Eyvind. 'I'll give you everything you want, and you can keep the silver if the workmanship is good; otherwise you must give it back to me.'

Hreidar was kept in a locked room, and there he worked at his craft. He'd not quite finished the article by the time King Harald arrived.

As we have already mentioned, Eyvind was far from unprepared for King Harald's arrival, and gave him a splendid feast. When they were drinking together, King Harald asked whether Hreidar was there. 'You'll earn my friendship if you hand him over to me,' he said.

Eyvind answered, 'He's not here now.'

'I know he's here,' said the king. 'There's no point in your denying it.'

'Even if he is, I'm not going to betray King Magnus by handing over to you the man he wants me to protect.'

With that he went out of the hall, and he'd only just left when Hreidar started hammering on the door and shouting he wanted to get out.

'Keep quiet,' said Eyvind. 'King Harald's here and wants to have you killed.'

But this didn't stop Hreidar from pounding on the door

and demanding to meet the king. Eyvind realized that he'd smash the door so he unlocked it, and said, 'You're as good as dead if you go in there.'

Hreidar stalked into the hall, went right up to the king, and greeted him. 'Sir,' he said. 'Don't be angry with me. I'm willing to carry out a dangerous mission if you want, even if it means risking my very life. I'll do anything you want me too. And here's something I'd like to give you as a present.'

Hreidar placed the object on the table in front of the king; it was a pig made of silver and gilded. The king looked at the pig, and said,' You're a really fine craftsman. I don't think I've ever seen anything of this kind so cleverly made.'

The pig was passed around from hand to hand, and the king said he'd make peace with Hreidar. 'It would suit me very well if you were to go on dangerous missions for me, you seem to be a strong, fearless man.'

Just then the pig was handed back to the king, and he picked it up to take a closer look at the workmanship. Then he realized that it was a sow with teats on it. He thought this must have been done in order to insult him,[4] so he threw the pig away, and said, 'The devil can have you. Take him and kill him, men.'

Hreidar picked up the pig and ran off. He made his way back to King Magnus and told him what had taken place.

Meanwhile, King Harald's men had got up and gone outside in search of him, determined to kill him. But when they came outside, they found Eyvind waiting for them with a large force, so they couldn't pursue Hreidar. King Harald left Eyvind, feeling far from pleased.

When Hreidar and King Magnus met, the king asked

4. The insult lies in the allusion to King Harald's father, Sigurd Sow (*sýr*), whose porcine nickname has very unheroic associations. See *Halldor Snorrason* below.

him what had happened. Hreidar told him the whole
story and showed him the pig. King Magnus looked closely
at it.

'What craftsmanship!' he said. 'But my uncle Harald
has taken revenge for lesser insults than this. You're a man
of great courage and ingenuity.'

Hreidar stayed at court for a time, and then he went to
see the king one day. 'I'd like you, Sir, to grant me a favour
I'm going to ask.'

'What's that?' asked the king.

'I'd like you to listen to a poem I've composed in your
honour, my lord.'

'Why not!' said the king.

Hreidar declaimed the poem. It was a strange composi-
tion, particularly at the beginning, but it got better towards the end.

When the poem was over, the king said, 'That's an odd
poem. Still, the last part is quite good. It seems to me your
poem is just like your own life. So far you've been a very
odd and eccentric person, but you'll improve the older you
get. As a reward for your poem I'm choosing a certain
little island off the coast of Norway. This I'll give you. The
island's small, it's true, but it's covered with lush grass and
the soil's fine.'

Hreidar said, 'This land of mine shall unite Norway and
Iceland.'

'I'm not sure how you'd get away with that,' said the
king. 'But this much I know, that many people will be
eager to buy it from you and pay for it in hard cash. I think
it would be better if you were to sell me the island; then it
won't be a bone of contention between you and those who
want to buy it off you. I don't think you should stay long
here in Norway. I know what King Harald will do to you
if he gets the chance, and he'll certainly do what he wants
if you stay here much longer.'

King Magnus bought the island from Hreidar and paid him with silver because he didn't want to risk his staying there any longer. Hreidar went back to Iceland and settled down in Svarfadardale with great success. His life turned out very much as King Magnus had predicted, for the older he grew, the better he became. He gave up all the foolery he'd indulged in when he was younger. He lived in Svarfadardale till old age, and a good many people are descended from him.

And so ends our story.

HALLDOR SNORRASON

1

HALLDOR SNORRASON had been with King Harald in Constantinople,[1] and came with him west from Russia to Norway. He was thought highly of and favoured by the king, staying with him the first winter in Norway at Kaupang. As winter wore on and spring was coming, traders started early preparations for their voyages, as there had been little trade between Norway and other countries because of hostilities with Denmark.[2]

Later in the spring, King Harald noticed that Halldor Snorrason had turned rather gloomy, and one day he asked Halldor what he had on his mind.

Halldor replied, 'I want to go to Iceland, Sir.'

The king said, 'Most people show more longing for home than you. But where's your outfit for the voyage? How are you going to spend your money?'

'My money's easily spent,' said Halldor, 'I own nothing but the clothes I'm wearing.'

'Then your long service with all its dangers hasn't been well rewarded,' said the king, 'but I'll provide you with a

1. Before he became joint ruler of Norway with his nephew King Magnus in 1046, King Harald had spent some time in Constantinople (c. 1035–44) where he commanded the Varangian Guard. *King Harald's Saga*, Penguin Classics, 1966, throws some interesting light on the relationship between Halldor and the king, both during their Varangian years and later. Halldor was the son of Snorri the Priest, one of the chieftains in *Ale-Hood*, see footnote on page 90 above.

2. This war between Norway and Denmark is described in *King Harald's Saga*, and it is mentioned in *Audun's Story*.

ship and cargo. Then your father will be able to see you haven't served me for nothing.'

Halldor thanked the king for his gifts. Some days later he went to see the king, who asked him how many crew he had signed on.

Halldor replied, 'All the young sea-faring men have already found themselves places on other ships. I haven't been able to hire a single hand, and I'm afraid the ship you gave me will have to stay behind here.'

The king said, 'In that case my gift won't be much use to you. We must wait and see what can be done about your crew.'

Next day the trumpet was sounded for a meeting in the town, and it was announced that the king wanted to address townsmen and traders. The king was late in coming to the meeting, and seemed to be very worried when at last he arrived. He said, 'We've heard that a war has broken out in our kingdom, east in Oslofjord. King Svein of Denmark is leading the Danish forces and means to finish us off, but we'll never give up our lands. That's why we can't permit any ship to leave our shores, till we have got from each of them what we need in the way of men and provisions. There's just one single exception: a small ship belonging to Halldor Snorrason which will be allowed to sail to Iceland. You'll no doubt find it hard we have to impose this on you when you're ready to sail. We'd certainly much rather there was peace and everyone could go where he wanted.'

Afterwards the meeting broke up, and a little later Halldor came to see the king. He asked Halldor how his preparations were getting on and whether he'd been able to get a crew.

Halldor replied, 'I've taken on rather too many; lots more than I needed came and asked me for a passage. They've been so eager that the house is in a shambles, and

I've had no peace day or night with all these men begging me to hire them.'

The king said, 'Keep the crew you've signed on for now, and we'll soon see what will happen next.'

The trumpet was sounded again the following day, and it was announced that the king wanted to speak to the traders. This time the king wasn't late in arriving for the meeting; he came before it started and seemed to be in a good temper.

He stood up and said, 'This time I've good news for you. There wasn't a word of truth in what you were told yesterday about the war. So we're giving every ship leave to go, whatever the destination wherever the captain wants to sail. Come back to us in the autumn, and bring us valuable gifts, and you'll have our friendship and favours in return.'

All the traders present were delighted to hear this, and thanked the king for what he'd told them.

Halldor went to Iceland that summer, and stayed the following winter with his father. Next summer he sailed abroad again and joined King Harald's court. But the story goes that he was less attached to the king than he'd been before, as he often stayed behind in the evening when the king went to bed.

2.

There was a man called Thorir England-Trader who'd long been a successful sea-going merchant. He'd visited a good many foreign lands and the gifts he'd brought the king were priceless. He was a retainer of King Harald, and now a very old man.

One day Thorir came to see the king and said, 'I'm an old man, as you must know, and I tire easily. I feel I can't keep up any longer with court customs, such as drinking toasts and doing whatever's expected of me. I'll have to look for another place to live, though I'd like most to stay with you.'

'This is easily settled, my friend,' said the king. 'Stay here at court, I give you leave to drink not a drop more than you want to.'

There was an Uplander called Bard; he was a fine man and still quite young. He was staying with King Harald too and was thought well of. These three were seated together: Bard, Thorir, and Halldor.

One evening the king happened to pass by the bench where these three men were drinking, and just at that moment Halldor passed on the horn. It was a huge stag-horn, and as it was transparent everyone could see Halldor had drunk more than his share against Thorir, who was a poor drinker.

The king said, 'It takes a long time to get to know a man properly. You keep cheating old men at drinking and chasing after whores at night, instead of following your king.'

Halldor said nothing, but Bard saw that he was in a fury about what the king had said. Early next morning Bard went to see the king.

'You're an early riser today, Bard,' said the king.

'I want to warn you, Sir,' said Bard. 'What you said to your friend Halldor last night was undeserved and spiteful. When you accused him of not drinking his share, he was drinking for Thorir who'd just given up the horn and would have returned it to the tray, had Halldor not drunk it for him. Besides, it's an utter lie about his running after loose women; all the same, most people would like him to serve you better.'

The king said he'd settle this with Halldor himself the next time they met. Bard went back to Halldor to tell him how friendly the king's words had been, and added that there was not the slightest reason for him to pay any attention to the king's outbursts. This is how Bard tried to put things right between them.

Time passed till Christmas, and relations between the king and Halldor remained rather cool. At Christmas, according to court custom, all breaches of etiquette were to be punished. And one morning during the festivities the time for the bell-ringing was changed, as the link-boys had bribed the bell-ringers to ring much earlier than was the custom. The result was that Halldor and many others were penalized, and were told to sit on the floor for the rest of the day and drink there. Halldor stayed in his seat, and when the penalty horn[3] was brought to him he refused to drink from it. This was reported to the king.

'It can't be true,' said the king, 'and I'm sure Halldor will drink up if I bring him the horn myself.' Then he took hold of the penalty horn and walked over to Halldor, who stood up to meet him. The king told him to drink from the horn.

Halldor answered, 'I don't think I should be penalized because you'd altered the bell-ringing just to be able to punish your retainers.'

The king said, 'You'll have to drink from the horn just like everyone else.'

'Sir,' said Halldor, 'maybe you'll have your way and make me drink, but I can tell you this much, that Sigurd Sow would never have tried to bully Snorri the Priest[4] like that.'

3. For breaches of etiquette at court the retainers were made to drink ale from a certain large horn, by way of punishment. The drinking-horn which was set aside for this purpose was called *vitis-horn* or 'penalty horn'.

4. Sigurd Sow was King Harald's father. For his nick-name see also *Hreidar The Fool*. Snorri the Priest was Halldor's father. See footnote on p. 109.

Then he stretched out his hand for the horn, picked it up and drank. The king stormed back to his seat.

On the eighth day of Christmas the retainers were paid. It was called *Harald's Mint* and consisted mostly of copper, less than half of it being silver. When Halldor got his pay, he emptied the coins into the lap of his cloak to examine them, and it seemed to him the silver wasn't very pure, so he swept down all the coins with his hand into the rushes on the floor.

Bard told him he was being stupid. 'The king's sure to take this as a personal insult and think that for all the pay he's given you he's been slighted.'

'There's nothing to be done about it now,' said Halldor. 'Anyhow, the risk is very small.'

3.

After Christmas the retainers started getting the ships ready, as the king meant to sail to the south of the country. When the king was ready to leave, Halldor still hadn't made any preparations. Bard said to him, 'Why aren't you getting ready, Halldor?'

'I don't want to,' said Halldor, 'and I'm not going. I can see now the king disapproves of me.'

'He'll certainly want you to go,' said Bard.

Bard went off to see the king, and told him Halldor wasn't getting ready. 'You'll not find it easy to fill his place in the prow,' he said.

'Tell Halldor I want him to come with me,' said the king. 'This coolness between us makes no difference.'

Bard went back to Halldor and told him the king had no intention of doing without his services, so eventually Halldor decided to go, and sailed with the king and his retainers south along the coast. One night during the voyage, Halldor said to the man at the helm, 'Veer a bit.'

The king said to the steersman: 'Straight on!'

Halldor said the second time: 'Veer a bit.'

The king repeated the same words as before.

Halldor said, 'You are heading straight for that rock.'

And that's what happened – the lower part of the prow was ripped off, and the other ships had to rescue them ashore. They pitched a tent there and started repairing the ship.

When Bard woke up he saw Halldor was tying up his hammock. He asked him what he was doing, and Halldor said he was going aboard a merchant ship lying at anchor near by. 'We're most likely parting for good now,' he said. 'This was the last straw, and I don't want the king to damage any more of his ships or valuables just to spite and humiliate me.'

'Wait a moment,' said Bard. 'I'm going to see the king again.'

When the king saw him, he said, 'You're up early, Bard.'

'Sir,' said Bard, 'I have to be. It's hard to keep peace between you. Now he's going to clear out and join another ship, and he'll sail off to Iceland in a temper. That's not a proper way for you to part, and I don't think you'll ever get another man as trustworthy as Halldor.'

The king said they could still be reconciled, he wasn't in the least put out. Bard went back to Halldor and repeated the friendly words the king had spoken.

Halldor answered, 'Why should I serve him any longer? I don't even get my pay without being cheated.'

Bard said, 'Don't talk like that. You ought to be satisfied with what the sons of noblemen are getting, and you didn't show much consideration yourself the last time when you spilled the silver into the straw. You must have realized the king regarded that as a gross personal insult.'

Halldor said, 'I'm not aware that I've ever cheated the king in my loyalty to him, as he's cheated me of my pay.'

'That's true,' said Bard, 'still, wait a bit. I'm going to see the king again.'

So that's what he did. When he met the king he said, 'Give Halldor his pay in refined silver, he's worth keeping.'

The king answered, 'Don't you think you're going rather too far to demand a different pay for Halldor than for landholders' sons, considering how outrageously he behaved last time he was paid?'

'Consider something else, Sir, of much more importance,' said Bard, 'Halldor is a brave man and you've been good friends for a long time. Think too of your magnanimity. You know Halldor's temper and stubbornness, and it would be to your credit to honour him.'

'Give him the silver then,' said the king.

That was done, and Bard went back to Halldor with twelve ounces of refined silver, and said, 'Can't you see now that you get everything from the king if you only ask for it? He's willing to give you anything you want.'

Halldor said, 'I'm not staying any longer on the king's ship. So if he wants me to stay on, he'll have to give me a ship of my own.'

Bard said, 'It's not really the thing for landholders to give up their ships to you. Now you're starting to ask far too much.'

Halldor said he wouldn't stay on unless he got what he was asking for. Bard told the king what Halldor was demanding. 'If the rest of the crew are as reliable as Halldor you can depend on his ship, sure enough.'

The king said, 'I know people think this request very unreasonable but I'm going to do something about it.'

There was a landholder, a man called Svein of Lyrgja, in command of one of the ships, and the king asked him to come and talk things over. 'You're a man of noble blood, as everyone knows,' said the king. 'That's why I want you to be on my ship, and I'll get someone else to take charge of yours. You're a very shrewd man, and I'd like to have the benefit of your advice.'

Svein said, 'Up till now you've always talked things over with others rather than me whenever you needed advice, and I'm not all that good at giving it either. Who do you mean to give my ship to?'

'Halldor Snorrason is to have it,' said the King.

Svein said, 'I'd never have thought you'd let an Icelander take over my command.'

The king said, 'His family's as distinguished in Iceland as yours here in Norway, and it's not all that long since the people of Iceland were Norwegians.'

The king got his way, Halldor took over the ship, and they sailed on their way east to Oslo calling in on a number of feasts.

4.

One day when the king and his men, including Halldor, were drinking in the royal chambers, the men keeping watch over Halldor's ship came bursting into the room, every one of them soaking wet. They said Svein and his men had seized the ship and thrown them overboard. Halldor got to his feet, went up to the king and asked if he was to have the ship as the king had promised. The king said he meant to keep his promise. He called on his retainers and told them to man six ships with a treble crew on each and go with Halldor. They chased after Svein, and he retreated before them up to the land, and ran ashore. Halldor and his men took the ship and went back to the king.

Late in the summer, when all the feasts were over, the king sailed north along the coast to Trondheim.

Svein of Lyrgja sent a message to the king telling him that he wanted to surrender his claim to the ship and give himself up to the king. He said he wanted only the king to settle the issue between Halldor and him, and that he'd accept the verdict, whatever it was. But Svein also said he'd prefer to buy the ship if the king didn't object. When the king realized how eager Svein was to refer the whole issue to him, he decided to settle it to suit both parties. So he asked Halldor to sell him the ship and offered a good price for it to give it back to Svein. The king bought the ship, and Halldor was paid in cash. The whole price was paid then and there, except for half an ounce of gold.[5] Halldor didn't press for its payment, and it stayed outstanding.

The winter passed, and in the spring Halldor told the king he wanted to go back to Iceland in the summer, so it would be handy for him if he could be paid the rest of the ship's price. But the king didn't like him asking for the money and was rather evasive about the payment, though he didn't forbid Halldor to leave. Halldor got his ship ready in the river Nid, and then brought it out to Brattaeyr. They were all set to leave, and the wind was fair.

Late in the evening Halldor went into town with several companions, fully armed. They made straight for the house where the king and his queen were sleeping, and Halldor went in while his companions waited outside. He made a lot of noise with his weapons as he entered the building. This woke up the queen and king who asked who was breaking in on them in the middle of the night.

'Halldor is here, ready for the voyage; the wind is fair, and the time's come to settle your debt,' he said.

'I can't do it in such a hurry,' said the king. 'We'll pay tomorrow.'

'I want it here and now,' said Halldor, 'and I'm not

5. Half an ounce of gold was the equivalent of the price of about 16 milch cows.

leaving till I get it. I know your moods well enough to realize what you must be thinking about the way I'm claiming my money. It doesn't matter at all what you keep promising now, I'll never trust you again. I doubt if I'll ever get a better chance, so I'm making the most of it now that I've got the upper hand. I see the queen's wearing a solid gold ring. Give it to me.'

'We must get the scales and weigh it first,' said the king.

'No need for that,' said Halldor. 'I'll take it as my due, and you're not going to fob me off this time. Hand it over right away.'

'Give him the ring,' said the queen. 'Can't you see the way he's standing over you, the killer?' She took the ring off her finger and gave it to Halldor. He accepted it, thanked them both for the payment, and bade them good-bye, 'I'm on my way,' he said.

Then he went outside and told his companions to run as fast as they could down to the ship. 'I'm not hanging round much longer in this town,' he said. They did as he told them, reached the ship, and hoisted sail at once, while others looked after the tow-boat, and still others heaved in the anchor, everyone doing his very best. As they were getting under way they heard the loud blaring of trumpets in the town, and the last thing they saw were three long-ships chasing them. But they made their escape out to the open sea, and their pursuers lost sight of them. The wind was still fair, and Halldor set course for Iceland. The king's men turned back when they realized Halldor had reached the open sea.

5.

Halldor Snorrason was tall and handsome, an exceptionally strong and brave fighting man. King Harald gave him a testimony, that of all the men who'd served with him, Halldor was the one who was least troubled by a sudden turn of events, whether it meant danger or good news. Halldor wasn't moved one way or the other. He wouldn't eat, sleep or drink more or less than was his custom, whether things were going well or badly for him.

Halldor was a man of few words, but he used to speak abruptly and frankly, and could be sharp and sarcastic. He was always self-willed, no matter whom he was dealing with, which infuriated King Harald who had plenty of other men to serve him. And that's why they got on so badly after Harald became king of Norway.

After Halldor came to Iceland he became a farmer at Hjardarholt and a few years later King Harald sent him a message to come to Norway and stay with him. The king said Halldor would be given as much honour as before, and should he accept the invitation and come to Norway the king would give him a position higher than that of any man not nobly born.

When Halldor received the message, he said, 'I shan't be visiting King Harald again, so let each of us just hold what he has. I know his temper well enough to realize that he'll keep his promise and not put anyone above me if I go to see him, for he'd put me on the highest gallows if he could have it his way.'

The story goes that when King Harald was growing old, he sent another message to Halldor, asking him to send him some fox furs; the king meant to use them on his bed because he needed the extra warmth. When Halldor got word from the king, his first comment was: 'The wakeful cock must be getting old now.' But he sent him some furs.

Halldor and King Harald never met after their parting in Trondheim, though they'd taken rather scant leave of each other at the time. Halldor farmed at Hjardarholt for the rest of his life and lived to be an old man.

AUDUN'S STORY

THERE was a man in the Westfjords called Audun; he was not well off and worked as a farmhand for a kinsman of his, a man called Thorstein.

One summer a ship put in at Vadil and its captain, Thorir, took lodgings with Thorstein, since he could provide the best accommodation. Audun gave the captain useful advice and helped him to sell his merchandise to people he knew who could be trusted to pay. The captain offered to pay him back for his help, and Audun decided to travel abroad with him. Thorir said he was welcome to be a passenger on his ship.

Audun told Thorstein what he'd decided to do, and said that when he'd sold the sheep and paid in advance for his mother's food and lodgings over the next three years – she was staying with Thorstein – he'd still be left with three marks of silver.[1] Thorstein said he seemed likely to have his share of good luck.

In the autumn Audun sailed abroad with Thorir, and at the end of the voyage Thorir invited him to come and stay in More, where he had a farm; it was very pleasant there.

Thorir asked Audun what he intended to do. 'I'd like you to know what I have in mind myself. I'm going to Greenland, and you're welcome to join me.'

Audun said he would like to go, and they went to Greenland the following summer. They put in at Eiriksfjord, and all the richest people on board took lodgings

1. Three marks of (unrefined) silver was equivalent to the value of six milch cows.

there, but the rest of them – including Audun – travelled
to the Western Settlement to look for somewhere to stay.[2]

Among the Greenlanders there was a hunter called
Eirik, and he captured a magnificent polar bear. When
Audun heard about it, he offered to buy the bear, but the
hunter said it wouldn't be wise of him to spend all his
money on the bear. 'I know you've only just about enough,'
he said.

Audun said that didn't bother him in the least and
bought the bear with all he had. Afterwards he went back
to Norway with Thorir, who once more invited him to
stay, but Audun said he'd try to get a passage on a cargo
boat and sail south to Denmark as he meant to give the
bear to King Svein Ulfsson.[3]

Thorir said it would be taking a great risk to travel
with something as valuable as that, 'considering the great
war going on between King Harald and King Svein.'

Audun travelled south, and when he reached Horda-
land, he found that King Harald[4] was attending a feast
there. The king was told a magnificent bear had been
brought, and he sent for the owner. Audun presented
himself before the king and greeted him.

The king returned the greeting and said, 'Do you have
anything valuable?'

Audun said yes, he had a bear.

'Will you sell me this beast at the price you paid for
it?' asked the king.

Audun said he wouldn't.

2. The Icelandic colony in Greenland was founded c. 985 A.D.
There were two distinct settlements, both on the west coast; the
Western Settlement was the more northerly of the two. See *The
Vinland Sagas*, Penguin Classics, 1965.

3. King of Denmark 1047–74. See *King Harald's Saga*, Penguin
Classics, 1966, and *Knytlinga Saga*.

4. King Harald Hardradi, see p. 109 above.

'It wasn't a fair offer, anyhow,' said the king. 'But will you sell me the bear at double the price you paid for it? Then you'd make a profit, as of course you should, since you say you bought it with everything you had.'

Audun said he wouldn't.

'Will you make me a present of it then?' asked the king.

Audun said he wouldn't and the king asked him what he meant to do with the bear.

Audun said, 'I'm planning to travel south to Denmark to give the bear to King Svein.'

The king asked, 'Are you really so stupid that you don't know this country's at war with Denmark? Or do you think you're so much luckier than everyone else that you can take a precious thing like this where even harmless people carrying nothing with them can hardly manage to travel?'

Audun said, 'It's up to you to decide what will happen to my expedition. Naturally, I've often heard about this bitter fighting between King Svein and yourself, but maybe I won't get hurt.'

The king said, 'I think it'll be best to let you get on with your journey – it could be good luck will come your way. But I want you to do me a favour: let me know how the journey turns out.'

Audun gave his promise. He set out and travelled south along the coast, then east to Oslofjord and from there across to Denmark. When he arrived he didn't have a penny and had to start begging food for himself and the bear. One evening he met a man called Aki, one of King Svein's stewards. Audun told him about his travels and asked him to give him food for the bear. Aki offered to sell him some, but Audun said he had nothing to pay with. 'I'd very much like to give the bear to King Svein.'

The steward said, 'I want a half-share in the bear. You must know it won't live long if no one helps you.'

Realizing the predicament he was in, Audun accepted the offer and sold Aki a half-share in the bear. Then they set out to see the king, with a large crowd following them. The steward and Audun came up to the royal table and greeted the king. He asked Audun what country he came from.

Audun said, 'I'm an Icelander, but I've just arrived from Norway, and before that I was in Greenland. I'd hoped to present you with this bear I bought with everything I had. I met King Harald, and he gave me leave to travel where I wanted after he made me an offer for the bear that I wouldn't take. But, my lord, when I came to see this man Aki my last penny had been spent; I was dying of hunger, and so was the bear. Now the gift's been spoiled. Aki wouldn't help me or the bear unless he got a half-share in it.'

The king asked, 'Is the man telling the truth, Aki?'

'Everything Audun has said was true', said Aki, 'and that's why I wanted him to have the other half.'

'You were a little man, Aki, and I made you great,' said the king; 'yet you thought it proper to stand in the way of this man who wanted to give me a priceless gift which he'd paid for with all he had. Even King Harald, our enemy, saw fit to let him travel in peace. You deserve to be put to death. Leave this land at once, I never want to set eyes on you again. But as for you, Audun, I feel just as much in your debt as if you'd given me the entire bear. You're a welcome guest and you must stay here for a long time.'

Audun accepted the invitation. However, one day he said, 'I want to leave, my lord.'

The king was slow to reply, and eventually he asked what Audun had in mind. Audun said he wanted to go on a pilgrimage to Rome.

'I'd have been offended if your reason hadn't been so

noble,' said the king. 'I'll give you money, and arrange for
you to travel with some other pilgrims.' Then he asked
Audun to come and see him on his way back.

Audun travelled to Rome. On his journey back he fell
ill and grew terribly haggard. All his money was gone so
he took to begging and was very thin and miserable when
he came back to Denmark and arrived at Easter at the
king's residence. Audun was too timid to come forward
and hid in a corner of the church. He meant to approach
the king as he returned from Vespers, but when he saw the
king and his courtiers in their elegant attire, he couldn't
muster courage to step forward.

The king went to his banquet in the palace, and Audun
had something to eat outside the church, as is the custom
of pilgrims before they throw off their staff and scrip.
Audun made up his mind to speak to the king when he
went to Compline, yet hard as he'd found it earlier in
the evening, it seemed much harder now when the courtiers had been drinking. But as they were going inside, the
king noticed this man and realized he hadn't had the
courage to come forward to speak to him.

So when the courtiers had gone inside, the king turned
back and said, 'The man who wants to see me can come
forward now.'

Audun came forward and fell at the feet of the king, who
could hardly recognize him. The king seized him by the
hand to welcome him. 'You've changed,' he said.

The courtiers started laughing at Audun, but the king
told them not to. 'He's provided better for his soul than
you have.'

Then a bath was prepared for Audun, and the king gave
him a set of his clothes which he'd worn during Lent. The
king invited Audun to stay on and become his cup-bearer.

Audun said, 'It's a generous offer, my lord, but I'm going
back to Iceland.'

'That's a strange choice,' said the king.

Audun said, 'I couldn't bear the thought of living here in luxury, while out in Iceland my mother is scraping a beggar's existence; time's up and the money I provided for her's finished.'

The king said, 'You must be a lucky man. It's the only reason you could give for wanting to leave, without offending me. But you'll stay with me until the ships are ready to sail.' Audun accepted gladly.

One day late in the spring, they went down to the harbour where ships were being fitted out for voyages to various countries in the Baltic, and to Saxony, Sweden and Norway. They came at last to a splendid ship which was being fitted out.

'What do you think of this ship?'

'It's a fine one,' said Audun.

The king said, 'I want to give you this ship in return for the bear.'

Audun thanked him for the gift.

A little later, when the ship was ready, the king said, 'Since you're determined to go, I shan't try to keep you back. I've been told that long stretches of the coast of Iceland are harbourless and dangerous for shipping, so your ship could be wrecked and the cargo lost. If that happened you'd have little to show that you'd visited King Svein and given him a most valuable gift. So here's a leather purse for you – it's full of silver – and you won't be penniless as long as you have this money. However, you might possibly lose this money too, and then you'd still have little proof that you'd visited King Svein and given him everything you owned.'

Then the king pulled a splendid bracelet off his arm and gave it to him.

'Should the worst come to the worst and you wreck your ship and lose your money,' the king continued, 'you will not be quite penniless when you get ashore if you keep the bracelet, and it will serve as proof that you've visited King Svein. But should you owe some highborn person a great favour, I think it would be a good idea for you to give him the bracelet. It suits a man of noble birth. Farewell!'

Audun sailed off and took the usual route through Ore Sound, north along the coast, until he reached the port where King Harald was in residence. This time Audun needed many hands to help him. He went to see the king and greeted him. The king received Audun cordially and invited him to join him in a drink, which Audun accepted.

'Did you give King Svein the bear?' asked the king.

'Yes, my lord,' said Audun.

'How did he repay you?' asked the king.

'First, he accepted my gift,' said Audun.

'I'd have repaid you in that way, too,' said the king. 'Did he reward you further?'

'He gave me provisions and a lot of money to go on a pilgrimage to Rome,' said Audun.

'King Svein gives money to a good many people, even to those who don't bring him priceless gifts, and I'd have given you such money, too,' said the king. 'What else did he give you?'

'He invited me to stay at his court when I came back from Rome, a beggar more dead than alive,' said Audun, 'and he gave me the clothes he'd worn during Lent.'

'I think it's no more than proper he shouldn't have starved you or denied you the use of his Lenten clothes,' said the king. 'One can easily treat beggars to that sort of thing, and I would have done the same. Was there anything else?'

'He invited me to become his cup-bearer,' said Audun.

'That was a great honour,' said the king, 'and I'd have done the same. What else did he repay you with?'

'He gave me a trading ship fully rigged and loaded with the finest cargo to come to this country.'

The king said, 'That was very generous of him, and just what I'd have done. When did he stop repaying you?'

Audun said, 'He gave me a large purse, full of money, and said I wouldn't be penniless even though I wrecked my ship off Iceland.'

The king said, 'That was really generous, and more than I'd have done. I'd have thought I'd settled my debt when I'd given you the ship, whatever happened to it afterwards. Did he then stop rewarding you?'

Audun said, 'He gave me this bracelet and said I might possibly lose the rest of my possessions but that I wouldn't be penniless as long as I kept the bracelet. He asked me not to give it away unless I felt so much in debt to a high-born person I felt I must give him the bracelet. Now I've found such a man, for you could easily have had me put to death, my lord, and confiscated my precious bear. But you let me go in peace although other people were not free to travel. I owe my good fortune to you.'

The king said, 'King Svein has very few equals indeed, although he and I have never got on well together. I accept the bracelet you give me, and you must stay with me here. I'll make sure your ship is made ready and I'll provide you with all you need for the voyage.'

Audun accepted the offer, and when he was ready to put out again, the king said, 'I'm not going to give you any expensive presents, but accept this sword and cloak.' Both were splendid gifts.

Audun sailed to Iceland in the summer and made land in the Westfjords. He became a man of great good fortune. He had splendid progeny. Thorstein Gyduson and many other good men are descended from him.[5]

5. Thorstein Gyduson died in 1190.

IVAR'S STORY

A MAN called Ivar was staying at the court of King Eystein.[1] Ivar was an Icelander, well-born and intelligent and a good poet.[2] The king thought very highly of him, and his fondness for Ivar is borne out by the following episode.

Ivar had a brother called Thorfinn, who also went to Norway to visit the court of King Eystein. Thorfinn had the benefit of his brother's popularity, but soon found it very trying not to be considered his equal and to have to depend on his brother's position. As a result Thorfinn grew discontented with court life and decided to return to Iceland.

Before the brothers parted, Ivar asked Thorfinn to take a message to a woman called Oddny, Jon's-daughter, telling her to wait for him and not to marry anyone else, for he loved her more than any other woman.

Thorfinn put out to sea, and had a good passage. He decided to propose to Oddny and married her himself. When Ivar arrived in Iceland some time later and heard about this, he felt his brother had played a cruel trick on him. Ivar was very unhappy and went back to Norway, where he stood as high in favour with the king as ever before.

As time went on, however, Ivar's anguish only grew worse. The king noticed this and summoned Ivar to his presence, to ask him why he was so distressed.

1. King Eystein Magnusson of Norway (d. 1122).
2. Ivar was a well-known Court Poet who lived for some time in Norway. Some of his poetry is still preserved.

'When you were staying with us in the past, you used to entertain us a great deal with your conversation. We don't ask you this question because we're afraid we have wronged you; and you're too intelligent a man to imagine a slight where none exists. Will you please tell us what's the matter with you.'

'What troubles me, my lord, is something I may not disclose,' said Ivar.

'Then we'll guess it,' said the king. 'Is there someone here whose presence offends you?'

'No, my lord, it's not that,' said Ivar.

'Do you feel we show you less honour than you'd wish?' asked the king.

'No, my lord, it's not that,' said Ivar.

'Is there anything you've seen in this country that you covet?' asked the king.

Ivar said no.

'The guessing grows harder,' said the king. 'Are there any estates you wish for?'

Ivar said no.

'Is there a woman in your own country you're pining for?' asked the king.

'Yes,' said Ivar.

'Then put your sorrow aside,' said the king. 'When spring comes, you'll go to Iceland, and we'll give you money and letters under our royal seal to her guardians. We don't know of anybody who wouldn't wish to act in accordance with our friendly words or with our royal threats, and marry this woman to you.'

'It's impossible, my lord,' said Ivar.

'No,' said the king, 'it's not impossible, we'll go further still, and even if she's already married we'll obtain her for you if that's what you desire.'

'It's a harder problem than that, my lord,' said Ivar. 'The woman's already married to my brother.'

'We must think of something else then,' said the king. 'I know what. After Christmas we'll be making our royal tour, and you shall come with us. You'll meet many gracious women, and as long as they're not of royal blood, we'll obtain any one of them for you.'

Ivar said, 'My lord, my difficulty's even more acute than that. Whenever I see a beautiful woman I'm reminded of the one I love, and my grief's redoubled.'

The king said, 'Then we shall give you the authority and estates we've already offered, and you can devote yourself to them.'

'I have no heart,' said Ivar.

'Then we shall give you money,' said the king, 'and you can travel wherever you wish.'

Ivar said he didn't want that either.

'Our problems grow worse,' said the king, 'for now we've tried everything we know. There's only one suggestion left, of very little value compared with our previous offers, but it's hard to guess what will be for the best. Come to me every day before the tables are cleared, when I'm not engaged in matters of state, and I shall talk with you. We'll talk about this woman to your heart's content for as long as you wish, and I'll devote my time to it. Sometimes a man's grief is soothed when he can talk about his sorrows. And I also promise you that you'll never leave my presence without some gift.'

'Yes, my lord, that's what I'd like to do,' said Ivar, 'and thank you for your consideration.'

And now, whenever the king was not engaged in matters of state, he would talk with Ivar about this woman. The plan succeeded, for Ivar's grief was cured sooner than he'd hoped; his happiness came back, and all his old cheerfulness returned to him.

And he remained with King Eystein.

LIST OF PERSONAL NAMES

Ivar (Ingimundarson), a court poet, 129–31

Magnus Olafsson, king of Norway (d. 25 October 1047), 94–108

Oddbjorg Skjoldolf's-Daughter, wife of Hrafnkel, 36

Oddny Jon's-daughter, 129

Ore-Bjorn, father of Thorkel Fringe, 83

Rannveig, wife of Bjarni of Hof, 76–7

Sam Bjarnason, of Leikskalar, 38, 44–63, 65–70

Sighvat Hallsteinsson, of Vidivellir, 64

Sigurd Sow, ruler of Ringerike in Norway, father of King Harald Hardradi, 113

Skapti Thoroddsson, of Hjalli, Lawspeaker of the Althing (d. 1030), 83, 85–9

Snorri Hallsteinsson, of Vidivellir, 64

Snorri the Priest, of Helgafell and Tongue (d. 1031), 83, 90, 113

Starri of Goddale, 90

Steingrim, 90

Svein of Lyrgja, a landholder in Norway, 116–18

Svein Ulfsson, king of Denmark (d. 28 April 1074 or 1076), 110, 123–8

Thorarin, of Sunnudale, a retired viking, 72–4, (78), 79–80

Thorbjorn, of Hol, father of Einar, 38, 43–52, 54, 61

Thord, one of Bjarni's servants, 72–4

Thord Gellir, father of Eyjolf, 83

Thord Hrolfsson, of Hrolfsstead, 64

Thord Thorgrimsson, brother of Hreidar, 94

Thordis Thorolf's-daughter, 49

Thorfinn, brother of Ivar, 129

Thorgeir Thjostarsson, of Thorskafjord, a chieftain, 49–61, 70

Thorhall, one of Bjarni's servants, 72, 75–6

Thorhall Ale-Hood, of Thorhallsstead, a farmer and an ale-brewer, 82–90, 93

Thorir, a Norwegian skipper, 121–2

Thorir England-Trader, a member of King Harald's household, 111–12

Thorir, son of Hrafnkel, 36, 71

Thorkel Fringe, a chieftain, 83, 89

Thorkel Eiriksson, a chieftain, 90

List of Personal Names

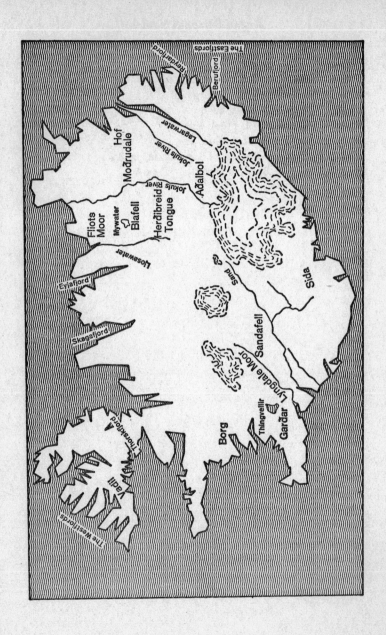

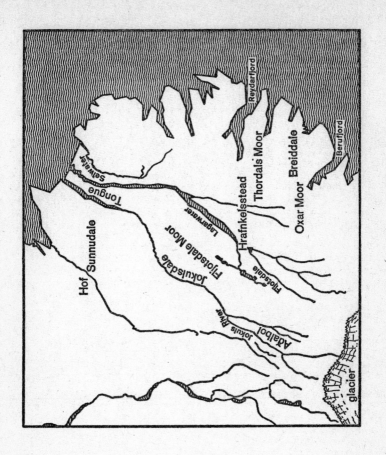

FOR THE BEST IN PAPERBACKS, LOOK FOR THE 🐧

In every corner of the world, on every subject under the sun, Penguin represents quality and variety – the very best in publishing today.

For complete information about books available from Penguin – including Puffins, Penguin Classics and Arkana – and how to order them, write to us at the appropriate address below. Please note that for copyright reasons the selection of books varies from country to country.

In the United Kingdom: Please write to *Dept E.P., Penguin Books Ltd, Harmondsworth, Middlesex, UB7 0DA.*

If you have any difficulty in obtaining a title, please send your order with the correct money, plus ten per cent for postage and packaging, to *PO Box No 11, West Drayton, Middlesex*

In the United States: Please write to *Dept BA, Penguin, 299 Murray Hill Parkway, East Rutherford, New Jersey 07073*

In Canada: Please write to *Penguin Books Canada Ltd, 2801 John Street, Markham, Ontario L3R 1B4*

In Australia: Please write to the *Marketing Department, Penguin Books Australia Ltd, P.O. Box 257, Ringwood, Victoria 3134*

In New Zealand: Please write to the *Marketing Department, Penguin Books (NZ) Ltd, Private Bag, Takapuna, Auckland 9*

In India: Please write to *Penguin Overseas Ltd, 706 Eros Apartments, 56 Nehru Place, New Delhi, 110019*

In the Netherlands: Please write to *Penguin Books Netherlands B.V., Postbus 195, NL–1380AD Weesp*

In West Germany: Please write to *Penguin Books Ltd, Friedrichstrasse 10–12, D–6000 Frankfurt/Main 1*

In Spain: Please write to *Longman Penguin España, Calle San Nicolas 15, E–28013 Madrid*

In Italy: Please write to *Penguin Italia s.r.l., Via Como 4, I-20096 Pioltello (Milano)*

In France: Please write to *Penguin Books Ltd, 39 Rue de Montmorency, F-75003 Paris*

In Japan: Please write to *Longman Penguin Japan Co Ltd, Yamaguchi Building, 2–12–9 Kanda Jimbocho, Chiyoda-Ku, Tokyo 101*

FOR THE BEST IN PAPERBACKS, LOOK FOR THE

PENGUIN CLASSICS

ANTHOLOGIES AND ANONYMOUS WORKS

The Age of Bede
Alfred the Great
Beowulf
A Celtic Miscellany
The Cloud of Unknowing and Other Works
The Death of King Arthur
The Earliest English Poems
Early Christian Writings
Early Irish Myths and Sagas
Egil's Saga
King Arthur's Death
The Letters of Abelard and Heloise
Medieval English Verse
Njal's Saga
Seven Viking Romances
Sir Gawain and the Green Knight
The Song of Roland

FOR THE BEST IN PAPERBACKS, LOOK FOR THE 🐧

PENGUIN CLASSICS

Bashō	**The Narrow Road to the Deep North**
	On Love and Barley
Cao Xuequin	**The Story of the Stone** *also known as* **The**
	Dream of the Red Chamber (in five volumes)
Confucius	**The Analects**
Khayyam	**The Ruba'iyat of Omar Khayyam**
Lao Tzu	**Tao Te Ching**
Li Po/Tu Fu	**Li Po and Tu Fu**
Sei Shōnagon	**The Pillow Book of Sei Shōnagon**
Wang Wei	**Poems**

ANTHOLOGIES AND ANONYMOUS WORKS

The Bhagavad Gita
Buddhist Scriptures
The Dhammapada
Hindu Myths
The Koran
New Songs from a Jade Terrace
The Rig Veda
Six Yuan Plays
Speaking of Śiva
Tales from the Thousand and One Nights
The Upanishads

THE GREAT ICELANDIC SAGAS

Njal's Saga

Translated by Magnus Magnusson and Hermann Pálsson

This magnificent saga, written by an unknown author in the late thirteenth century, describes a fifty-year blood feud from its violent beginnings to its tragic end.

Laxdaela Saga

Translated by Magnus Magnusson and Hermann Pálsson

This saga, composed by an unknown author *c.* 1245, has always stirred the European imagination the most profoundly. Romantic in style, in taste and in theme, it culminates in a beautifully described triangle of love.

Orkneyinga Saga

Translated by Hermann Pálsson and Paul Edwards

Probably written around AD 1200 the *Orkneyinga Saga* is the only Norse saga concerned with what is now part of the British Isles. Beginning in the remote world of mythic origins and legends, it relates the conquest of the Northern Scottish Isles by the Kings of Norway during the great Viking expansion of the ninth century and the subsequent history of the Earldom of Orkney.

THE VINLAND SAGAS

Translated by Magnus Magnusson and Hermann Pálsson

The two medieval Icelandic sagas translated in this volume tell one of the most fascinating stories in the history of exploration – the discovery of America by Norsemen, five centuries before Christopher Columbus.